TRAINING POINTING DOGS

TRAINING POINTING DOGS

All the Answers to All Your Questions

Paul Long

NICK LYONS BOOKS

ACKNOWLEDGMENTS

I am deeply grateful to the friends who helped me to create this book; particularly to Wayland F. Richardson for editing my manuscript, and to Stanley B. Hinman Jr. on legal matters.

Paul Long

Many of the photographs in this book were taken by A. Hamilton Rowan, Jr.—specifically, those appearing on pages 7, 8, 13, 40, 41, 45, 46, 48, 60 and 88. The publishers wish to thank him and Mr. Denes Burjan for their assistance. Photographs on pages 5, 20, 25 and 62 (top) are by Howard Danner; those on pages 42 and 95 by J. Wallace Campbell.

Copyright © 1974, 1985 by Paul Long

Library of Congress
Catalog Card Number: 85-081198

ISBN: 0-941130-07-X (hardcover): 0-941130-08-8 (paperback)
Printed in the United States of America
10 9 8 7 6 5 4 3 2

TO ALL MY CANINE FRIENDS
who may disagree but cannot contradict.

FOREWORD

by A. Hamilton Rowan, Jr.,
   Director of Field Trials and Hunting Tests,
   The American Kennel Club

The importance of Paul Long's book is its straightforward, simple country honesty. I once met Paul Long at a field trial in New Jersey shortly after this book was first published in 1974. I had a chance then to chat with him—long enough to confirm my suspicions that here was a man who knew almost everything there was to know about training pointing dogs.

As a young boy in my native England, my father saw to it that an expert was available to give me all the answers to all my questions about country living. We lived on a dairy farm south of London. Our resident "Paul Long" was the middle-aged son of a Scottish gamekeeper, the many likes of which came to this country in the 1930's to impart their ingrained training smarts on the gun dog retrievers that had become the vogue of the wealthy Eastern estate owners.

James Pettigrew, whose primary job was to tend my parents' extensive flower and vegetable gardens, was a countryman in the purest sense of the word. Every day that I was home from boarding school, we would take long walks with his son through the adjoining fields and woods. At first, birds, flowers and trees were identified; animal tracks and trails studied; wild edibles gathered and, each spring, bird nests found and watched.

Later it was time for us to have a shooting dog. A Springer Spaniel pup was found, and her training begun.

From single-barreled .410's, we graduated to 12-gauge doubles under Pettigrew's ever watchful eye. "Judy" became an effective gun dog. By then, we were allowed to take her afield by ourselves, and game almost became a culinary staple. We were certifiable countrymen after ten incredibly meaningful years—my lifelong legacy from a superb countryman.

As a boy, Paul Long also received a countryman's legacy from Mike Seminatore—the legendary New England trainer of English Setter gun dogs. After graduating from high school, Long made dog training his life's work.

Is there any wonder, then, why Long should have gained the straight, commonsense knowledge about training pointing dogs after all these years? Although he is no literary stylist, his writing contains none of the puffery found in other dog-training books. His style enables Long to answer all your dog-training questions in eighty-four pages.

Each year, new books are written on the training of dogs—pointing dogs. Often the authors are new to the subject matter, and feature "new" training methods based, perhaps, on the latest research of some canine psychologist. It all makes for interesting and sometimes entertaining reading; but these books are not written by countrymen. They inevitably confuse the inexperienced dog owner, who is trying to train his equally confused dog. Above all else, they assume that training problems will never happen. Laboratory theories may look promising in the lab. However, they are of little use in a woodcock covert, or upon entering the bird field at a field trial.

What counts in the real world of bird dog training is knowledge gained from years and years of training, hunting, and field-training pointing dogs. The dogs themselves taught Long over the years just how to outsmart a dog; how to anticipate its next move; how to mold your pup into the likeness of your needs. And, in this latter regard, here is what usually happens. Along the way, and just when you are ready to compliment yourself on a training job well done, that sparkling canine mind will suddenly taunt you with a major behavioral problem. He may be stealing points, or flagging on point; or, perhaps, not even pointing his birds anymore. The development of any one of these problems (and many others) will cause most amateur trainers to seek psychiatric, psychic or spiritual succor—albeit for themselves, because such counsel is not available for their "psychotic" dogs.

My advice to the amateur whose dog has placed him on the threshold of a nervous breakdown is to check Long's book, because one is sure to find that he has experienced the same problem— then, follow his old-fashioned, patent medicine cure. It will generally work.

Truly important about Long's book is its applicability not only to the upland game hunter and the competitive field trialer, but also to the participant in the new Hunting Tests for Pointing Breeds. (Tailored to the upland hunter, Hunting Tests are a new concept of testing dogs against a hunting performance standard in a non-competitive event. The program was pioneered by The American Kennel Club in 1984.)

A pointing dog that has been trained to carry out the bidding of its owner is always admired. The owner, however, with an unruly dog will be shunned as a hunting companion. At field trials, training inadequacies will leave a dog out of the ribbons, and at a hunting test it will fail to receive a qualifying score.

The responsibility for training a dog rests entirely with its owner, even though he may elect to have the job done professionally. The responsible owner of a pointing dog will always see to it that his dog receives sufficient training to suit his needs. To this end, Paul Long's book can be as indispensable as a check cord.

A. Hamilton Rowan, Jr.
Director of Field Trials and Hunting Tests
The American Kennel Club

February, 1985

Contents

1

Things to Ponder

What Kind of Puppy Should I Buy?

I have found fine bird dogs in all pointing breeds, and also disappointing dogs in all. Pick the breed that takes your eye and find out all you can about the ancestry of the puppy that appeals to you. If you want to win field trials, look for winners in his pedigree. If you are not interested in field trials and are just looking for a good dog to hunt over, find out how his parents performed under the gun. And then hope for the best. Great gun dogs come out of field trial lines and dogs with the range, style and vigor sought for in field trials appear where only a comfortable gun dog was wanted.

Much more important than picking the breed is picking a dog that fits your personality. Some dogs in all breeds are extroverts; others are introverts. If you are a no-nonsense individual, dislike petting an animal, and are not above giving a good thrashing, get a dog that will stand up to your personality, without cringing or showing fear, until you have it thoroughly trained. If, on the other hand, you object to any degree of punishment as a training aid, you should get a dog that thrives on affection and needs only a harsh voice or light correction to set it right.

1

And until you are sure of your dog's personality and your own, take the light approach.

How Do I Keep My Dog Happy?

The things a dog needs for basic contentment are:
Food
Clean water
A warm bed
Shade and warm sun
A little care
A little companionship

Companionship was mentioned last, but is not least. It need only be "Hello, boy" as you walk by. But, like a politician with a prospective voter, let him know that you are glad to see him, and give him recognition.

What Should I Feed My Dog?

I give my opinion only as a dog trainer and not as a dietician, but you can check it with your veterinarian. You cannot give a healthy dog anything better for him than a good brand of dry dog food—meal, kibbled or nuggets—mixed with water. Much research has gone into the formulation of these foods, and probably, on the whole, the dogs that eat them have a better balanced diet than their masters. Some of the same makers and others have fancied up their foods to look more appealing to the human eye, but this makes little difference to the dogs. Some makers of canned dog food boast that their product is "all meat" and therefore, presumably better for your dog. If you check the analyses printed on the labels you may find that the all-meat product has much less of the protein that an active dog needs than the average dry food.

Should I Try to Train Him Myself?

By all means. You'll get to know your dog better and more about your own limitations in ability and temperament. You will also get a better appreciation of the problems a professional trainer has to solve in turning out a well trained dog.

Frankly, it's your dog. You bought him for your pleasure. If you are not successful, who cares except you? There's the rub. You do care. Since you care, keep reading. I believe that anyone can train a bird dog if he will pay close attention to this book.

What Are the Main Things in Dog Training?

The basic rule of dog training is repetition, repetition, repetition, plus common sense. One nail at a time will build a house. Repetition will eventually produce a well trained dog.

Remember that dogs are like youngsters, with this difference. A puppy does not fully mature until it is about three years old, while young people do not until their late teens. This comparison can be carried a bit further. A puppy under a year old is like a child in his pre-school and kindergarten years, when a lot can be learned through informal training. When 12 months old the puppy is like a child entering grade school. He is ready for the formal disciplined schooling that will provide the base for all future progress. Failure to complete this training satisfactorily will always be a handicap. Not until he gets passing grades in this elementary schooling is he ready for the further education needed to fill his role in life ably and responsibly.

Remember also that until a dog performs satisfactorily in five different locations (unfamiliar areas for a hunting dog or different field trial courses for a field trial dog), your training cannot be considered complete.

Bear in mind, too, that every dog being trained is looking for what I call his escape hatch. The dog being taught to heel is walking quietly at your side. Suddenly he pulls away, or reverses the side he is heeling on. Your dog is pointing a bird. Suddenly he jumps in. You bring him back and command "Whoa". He jumps in again. You bring him back with more determination. He knows that you mean business, but he relaxes on point, wags his tail, or even lies down. You have given your puppy a workout and are bringing him back to the car. Suddenly he circles the car, maybe giving you a quick look, and takes off to hunt some more. All these dogs are seeking an escape hatch, a relief from training. A trainer must, from observation and instinct, anticipate these moves and thwart them before the dog can carry them out.

Again, dogs are like children. You tell your kids to go to bed. They start, but then decide that they need a glass of water, or something to eat, or to do their homework. That is their escape hatch. With dogs, as with children, firm insistence will bring recognition of the fact that it is your wishes, not theirs, that must be obeyed.

What Do I Need for Training?

Most of all you need the attitude that you are going to be a teacher, not a brute.

You also need a commanding voice, a whistle, and a place where you can work your dog, the larger the better, preferably several hundred acres.

If possible, a supply of wild game. If you live in pheasant country but the birds are scarce, I suggest that you strew a heavy feeding of scratch grain along roads near swampy areas. If birds are there it will hold them for weeks, and may draw others to the area. To supplement wild birds, you will need some pigeons and/ or quail. For pigeons and quail, it would be helpful if you could have a pigeon loft and quail recall pen.

For yard training you need mainly a leash, a cardboard tube from a roll of paper towels or foil wrapping, and several long check-cords. A 30-ft. cord will prove the most useful, but there are times when a shorter cord will do, and others when a 50-ft. cord will be advantageous. I recommend 3/8-in. nylon, burned or taped at the ends, for all. It runs smoothly through the cover, and its size minimizes snagging. Don't buy small-diameter nylon; it will burn your hand badly if you try to pick it up when it is running. Good cotton-covered clothesline or sash cord would be better in that respect but not as good as the 3/8-in. nylon from the standpoint of snagging.

For introducing your dog to the gun, it would be ideal to have an air rifle, a .22 rifle, and a .410 shotgun, to accustom the dog in easy stages to the boom of a large-gauge shotgun. But there are other ways of doing it. A cap pistol and a .22 blank pistol, used judiciously, will do. If training for field trials you should also have a .32 blank pistol, the minimum caliber permitted in some events.

You may also have need of a choke collar or spiked collar. A

Some of Paul Long's training tools, including, along with various fire-arms: field release cages, check cords, training collars, and electronic trainers, and such unusual aids as a cardboard tube, a soft drink bottle, and "Flush Away," (in center between rifles), an effective homemade bird releaser.

slingshot (if your aim is good) or electronic trainer will help you to correct a dog that disobeys beyond your reach.

It would also be nice to have a dog box for carrying your dog to and from the fields, a friend who will help you when teaching staunchness or backing, and an understanding spouse to look after your dog when you are away from home.

Mainly you need a strong desire to make your dog a success and ingenuity to think of acceptable substitutes for things beyond your reach.

Do You Advise Whipping as Discipline?

Consider for a minute. There is no animal, including man, that doesn't require a certain amount of pain to make a believer out of him. A dog is no exception. But when I say pain, I do not mean cruelty in any form.

To possess the nice things in life, a man must have a job, and this is the pain he endures for these comforts. A boy getting an education must do homework. This is the pain he must accept for the privilege. An athlete must practice, sweat, and maintain a rigorous schedule to keep fit. This is the pain he suffers for his moments of greatness.

The same holds true for a dog. If you say "No" to a dog, enforcing it, this is one form of pain. If it is necessary to shake his collar with the dog attached, this is the pain received for not obeying.

If the lash is applied merely to inflict physical pain, it is not the answer. What was the purpose of it? Was it only enough to instill fear that worse could follow if the command is not obeyed to your satisfaction?

A person who whips a dog out of sheer temper should give up dogs and take up boxing or, better still, get a henpecking wife.

The point to remember is this: the pain, whether it's your harsh voice, a shake of the collar, the electronic trainer or the lash, is to instill character and discipline. Whether your dog is an extrovert or an introvert, use only enough to have a well trained dog.

What Are the Four Most Important Words to a Dog?

There are other words that, as time goes on, you will use and your dog will learn to understand and obey, but the four most important ones are the four basic commands of yard training. When your dog has learned them you will get compliments on his obedience and your ability as a trainer. These words are:

WHOA—A dog that stops in his tracks when you say "Whoa" cannot get into trouble.

NO— To stop misbehavior.

HERE— To bring your dog in to you. You can use "Come" or his name, or use either command and his name.

HEEL— To have your dog walk quietly at your side.

Do Dogs Think?

Dogs have excellent memories. Their recall is terrific, but they do not think. Memory and instinct, not thought, guide their actions.

For example, your dog is lying on the hearth, enjoying the heat from the open fire. The fire dies down and the dog gets cold. If

The four most important words to a dog: "No" "Whoa . . ."

he could think, he would paw a piece of wood onto the fire from the nearby supply. Instead, he just curls up tighter, his instinctive way of keeping warm.

On the last day of hunting season your dog does well. He points staunchly, stays steady to wing and shot, and retrieves on command. On opening day of the next season, he tires a little sooner, but otherwise does just as well. He had memorized his training and your desires, and this, plus instinct, made him the same valuable dog. While kenneled he had thought up no new ways of doing things. He was guided by his recall of training and what you expect from him.

On the other hand, on the last day of the season your dog does well on a couple of finds. Then he overruns a bird and chases. The rest of the day he raises hell in general. On opening day of the next season he is just as bad. If he could think, he would realize that he was defeating the purpose of his being there. But he cannot think and nothing was done to revive his memory of

"... Here"

"Heel"

his training. His instinct to chase was stronger than his memory.

But now you have had enough. You catch the dog and discipline him by the means appropriate to this dog. A few tastes of this and once more he is the well trained dog he had been. Not because the dog thought about it, but because you had revived his recall of what was expected from him and the discomfort that follows failure to regard your wishes.

It's a good thing that your dog cannot think. If he could his mind would break down with the confinement that is his lot except when it suits your desires. It is good that living for the moment and basic comfort make him happy.

But *you* can think. Do that if your dog slips back in his training. Somehow, somewhere, some act of yours, or failure to act, is responsible.

Should I Buy An Electronic Trainer?

By all means. Used properly the electronic trainer can help you in many ways in your regular training and in correcting faults like chasing rabbits or even chicken killing. But if you buy one don't feel that to get your money's worth you have to press that button on every possible occasion. A very few uses at the right time can do you and your dog a world of good, while excessive use, or use at the wrong time, can do great harm. And the electronic trainer should never be used when the dog is approaching or pointing a bird on the ground.

Although in experienced hands the electronic trainer can be used in almost any stage of training, I recommend as little use as possible in yard training, especially for the inexperienced. Teach your dog the commands he is expected to obey by conventional means. When you are sure he understands and he persists in disobeying, the shocker can help you.

All dogs should be conditioned before the trainer is used on them. By conditioning I don't mean merely putting the dummy collar on them several days before the energized collar is used, although that is advisable. I mean that the dog has reached the point in training where he has some idea of what is expected of him and has learned that discipline follows disobedience. He has learned to accept milder forms of discipline and will accept this.

In his first experience with the collar he will be momentarily upset, but he will not be as completely bewildered, or possibly balky, as he might otherwise be.

There are numerous electronic trainers on the market, and you may have an opportunity to buy or borrow one previously used. Any will do if it will shock the dog when you want it to, and not shock it when you don't want it to. Some trainers, especially early models, are set off by short-wave-radio transmissions from walkie-talkies, planes and land vehicles. Some later models have a circuit to lock out interference but will shock a dog if you touch his collar, or even get very close to him, with this circuit switched on. Whatever trainer you buy or borrow, try it out with a test light, or better yet have a friend operate the transmitter and you hold the collar contacts in your hand. This will help you to know its capabilities and faults, if any.

All electronic trainers should be tested frequently with a test light before use. A trainer can fail by not administering a shock when you want it to, which makes it useless. But it can also fail by not terminating the shock when you release the switch button, which makes it worse than useless. Check for both types of failures. Before using a trainer on a day when a thunderstorm is approaching, test it to determine if the collar will be activated by distant lightning discharges. If it is, put the trainer aside until a better day.

Practice developing a light touch to avoid long shocks. Put the test light on the collar in a dimly lit room and experiment to learn how briefly you can hold down the transmitter button and still light the light. Most discipline requires only a brief prickle. Many collar users shock too long.

Later in this book you will find times when I recommend placing the collar not in the traditional place, around the dog's neck, but around his belly just ahead of his hindquarters. This is the place to have it if there is any chance the dog might be shocked while on a bird. Dogs are used to hitting briars and sticks when plunging through cover, and perhaps for that reason don't associate the prickle of the collar on the belly with the bird ahead as they are liable to do when shocked on the neck.

Can I Anticipate My Dog's Intentions?

Yes. A dog will telegraph by a dip of his tail if he is called and isn't going to heed the command. He will turn his head slightly if he is going to blink; that is, shy away from game. The eyes of a dog on point will protrude; he is waiting for the slightest movement of game or grass before jumping in to catch his quarry. A dog on point is in an hypnotic state until the bird flushes, when instinct takes over and commands him to catch the bird. The birdier the dog, the more his eyes will pop, and if he is a puppy, derby, or otherwise not thoroughly trained, watch out.

The slightest unnatural movement of your dog should set you to thinking hard, Why the movement?

Watching your dog closely will help you to make your dog look his best. Wait until he has reached the objective of his cast to blow your whistle or signal otherwise. A dog headed for an objective is not easy to turn; once there he is receptive to new orders.

A dog on a good running cast at breakaway may stop momentarily to relieve himself. Just before he finishes this chore he will look in your direction, and a command given at this precise moment will be obeyed. Field trials have been won or lost by this knowledge or the lack of it.

2

Pre-School

How Soon Should I Start Training My Puppy?

As soon as you get him. A puppy seven or eight weeks old is already starting to learn, and the more you work with him in the right way the more he will become *your* dog.

Even if he will be a kennel dog most of his life, try to bring him into the house or find another way to give him some time with people every day. It is puppies that spend their formative months in a kennel without human companionship that, no matter how well cared for otherwise, may turn out queer—manshy, afraid to come through the kennel door, unsafe with children, etc.

Of course you should not use harsh discipline on a baby dog, any more than you would on a human baby. Anyone who would should not be allowed to have either.

A puppy's attention span is short, but a lot can be taught to very young puppies in brief training sessions with plenty of romp and play in between. And the puppy is not only learning; he is learning to learn and to enjoy working with you.

He can be taught to come by saying "Come" or "Here", leaning down to the puppy's level, clapping your hands and then holding them wide in invitation. When he obeys, reward him with praise

Seven-week-old pups are old enough to be introduced to game birds. The handler is holding a hen pheasant.

and affection, even a tidbit at first. There will come a time, after you know he understands the command, when he will not obey because something else interests him more. Or he will come close and then jump away when you reach for him. It is your introduction to his escape hatch.

When this happens, put a six-foot cord on him. Call him again. If he balks or shies away, pick up the cord, smack him mildly with a rolled up newspaper, and gently pull him to you. Praise him lavishly when he comes without admonishment. Failure to come when called is a puppy's first test of whether obedience is really necessary. Nip his disobedience in the bud. A little mild chastisement now will save him harsher discipline later on.

A little puppy also quickly learns what "No" means if you say that disapprovingly as you stop him from doing whatever it is that he is doing wrong. Use only your voice the first few times you correct him, but if he persists use the rolled up newspaper. Puppies are quick to get the message.

Approval means a lot to a puppy. When he does right, make a lot of him. When he does wrong, let your voice show your disapproval. If your voice is not enough, use the rolled up newspaper. It reprimands without really hurting. Of course, as in disciplinary measures later on, how much you should use it depends on the temperament and reactions of your dog. Observe and use common sense.

Using these methods, you will be amazed at how much can be taught a very young puppy. But don't try to make a paragon of virtue of your puppy all at once. When he is doing well on one command, move on to the next one, and so on. Start any lesson with a brief review of what the puppy has already learned. Keep the sessions short and intersperse plenty of play and just fooling around.

This is not a recipe for winning puppy stakes in field trials. If you should enter your puppy, the judges may think he is lacking in ambition because he is paying too much attention to you. But it is a recipe for getting started with a little puppy that you will want to hunt to the gun. And it will develop a dog ripe for the finishing training required to produce a polished gun dog or—if he has the style, zest for hunting, and bird handling talents needed— a winner of field trial stakes for adult dogs.

One last word. If your puppy fails to obey, for example, the command of "No", don't keep saying "No, no, no" and go whack-whack-whack with the newspaper. One firm "No" and one smart whack, adjusted in force to the dog's age and temperament, will do you and him much more good.

How Do I Train My Puppy to the Leash?

Put a small collar on the puppy, with a ten or twelve foot leash or training cord attached. Turn him loose in a safe field or yard, letting go of the leash. After the puppy has run free for about twenty minutes, pick up the leash and follow him wherever he wants to go, within reason. When you wish to change direction, the puppy will probably fight the leash or balk. Slacken the leash, pet the dog and encourage him to move. Follow the puppy again. Several such lessons and he will go with the leash willingly.

Once the puppy is leash broken, tie him to some object and walk off thirty to fifty feet. The pup will probably object to being tied and fight the leash. Don't let him injure himself. Walk to the dog, pet him, and back off a few feet, repeating as necessary. Within a few minutes your puppy will be not only leash broken but accustomed to being tied, or to being kennel chained when the time comes for serious training.

Five lessons easily accomplish these two steps toward further training. And the puppy will have enjoyed every minute he was getting your undivided attention and affection.

Is Sight Pointing Good for a Very Young Puppy?

There is no great harm if no scent is involved. It makes you happy and it helps to develop the pup's pointing instinct. But don't cast out a bird with your fishpole. Cast out some small object. It will do just as well for a very young puppy, because little puppies point from sight, not scent.

Once a puppy begins to point from scent, he should not be allowed to sight point. If you let him, you are encouraging the dog not to stop on scent but to move in until he can see the game. Once he sees it, he will, at the slightest movement of the quarry, jump in to catch it.

No dog that keeps moving after scent until he can see the bird will hold birds on the ground for the handler to flush. This is one of the greatest faults amateurs create in their dogs, and it is hell to correct later on.

People rave about their puppies that are pointing at three or four months of age. It's nice, but why the praise? It is instinct, nothing that the owner did. Let's see the puppy pointing at eighteen months of age with all his character as the handler walks in to flush. Then the handler and the dog merit praise.

My Puppy Runs Off When I Want to Pick Him Up

This is good in one way because it indicates a puppy that loves to run and hunt, and he runs away because he doesn't want to stop. But it is an aggravating trait and should not be tolerated.

Try to avoid building this fault into your puppy. Don't let him come to think that every time he is called in the fun is over. Call him in several times during his run, pet and praise him, and then give him his freedom again.

If necessary, run him with a 10-foot cord dragging from his collar. Loosen the collar one hole so that the pup can slip it if he gets snagged out of your sight. The chance of snagging is slight if you use a 3/8-in. nylon cord burned or taped on the ends, but why take chances? When you return to the car and the pup runs around the car or by you, step on the rope and catch him. Pet him and put him in the car.

The electronic trainer will cure this fault very quickly, but I hesitate to recommend it to an inexperienced owner with a young puppy. You will have to be the judge of whether this method is right for you and your puppy.

Put the electronic collar on the dog before you let him loose, but leave the transmitter in the car so that you can't be tempted to use it for other reasons. Let the puppy have a good run. When you return to the car pick up the transmitter and call the dog in. If he refuses, or comes part way and dashes off again, shock him and call him again.

The fun will go out of him immediately. He will either come running to you, or bolt off, or stand in his tracks like a sullen bull calf.

If he comes running to you, your troubles are over, and you may never have to use the trainer again for this purpose.

If he bolts off, *do not shock him again.* Let the unpleasant sensation sink in and he will soon return voluntarily to circle the car. When he does, call him again. If he refuses or starts off again, shock him the second time. Now command him to you, but do not use an angry, high-pitched voice that will frighten the dog. Pet him and put him away.

If your puppy freezes in his tracks at the first shock, walk out, leash him and pet him, and lead him to the car. You have accomplished your primary purpose, catching the dog. Be satisfied with that for the time being.

On your next workout be prepared to repeat the same procedure. You may not have to use the shocker in this workout, but if you do I am sure that the puppy will be only too happy to come to your car when called thereafter.

Can I Teach My Puppy to Quarter?

Quartering, or criss-crossing in front of you, is easily taught to some dogs. In others it is hard to do. Most quartering dogs come from regions like Pennsylvania, New England or Michigan, where cover is heavy and game is, or at least used to be, relatively plentiful. In the South, Southwest and Western Canada, dogs have been developed to run the edges and cast out to likely objectives. Differences in topography and agricultural methods dictate the needs of gunners in a particular region, and dogs of the region have been bred to meet these needs.

So if your puppy comes from a line of dogs that has been bred for the wide open spaces, he may not adapt readily to the quartering you would like for small fields and heavy cover. However, in many of today's dogs there is an intermixture of strains, and the way to find out if your dog will take to quartering is by trying.

When you cast your dog off in the field and he, for example, goes to the right, you veer to the left and signal to your dog by voice, whistle or arm motion. Dogs are pretty clever at catching on to hand signals. When the dog veers to the left after your signal, you catch his attention by signaling again and veer to the right, continuing this procedure throughout the workout. Most dogs learn this quickly.

You may feel however that your dog is running too far out. If you are perceptive, it is not hard to tell whether your dog means to disobey you, or it is just not in his nature to run close.

Some dogs have the desire to go great distances yet keep in touch with the handler. A dog that runs wide but looks toward you to check your whereabouts before moving on to good looking cover is usually handling.

The dog that is refusing to handle will run wide, but will go up and down the same hedgerow many times or go off into swamps and woods on his own, checking on you just enough so that he will not lose contact completely. Coming from the rear, following your foot or horse tracks, is not obeying.

If your dog handles but runs too wide to suit your taste and you especially dislike this, think about trading him off and getting the kind of dog you want. It will be an uphill fight to make him into a close dog, and neither he nor you may be happy if you succeed.

How Do I Teach My Dog to Work on a Check-Cord?

Don't—as I have seen many beginners do—let the dog strain continuously at the end of the cord. As he nears the end of the training rope give a short staccato command—"Hup", "Hike", or even "Here" said more tersely than when calling the dog in, will do. Give a light jerk on the cord as you give the command and the dog will change direction. Repeat as needed and the dog will learn to range within the limits of the cord. This command will continue to serve you in the field long after check-cord days are over.

Do I Need to Use a Whistle?

Yes, even if your dog will be a close worker, he needs to learn whistle signals. There will be times when, because of a strong wind, heavy cover, or dips in the terrain, he cannot hear you especially if you hunt with a bell, and a whistle will penetrate where your voice will not.

You should have three different signals for three different commands—one, perhaps a couple of short toots, to send him on; another, perhaps one long blast, to catch his attention and turn him, and the third, perhaps repeated long blasts, to bring him in. You can devise your own personal whistle signals if you want to, but most dogs will recognize your whistle "voice" even when you are using the same make of whistle and the same whistle code as a fellow handler.

Teaching your dog whistle signals is the easiest of all your training assignments. Give him the go ahead signal when you turn him loose, and combine the other signals with voice commands the first few times. Your dog will quickly catch on.

How Do I Get My Puppy Birdy and Pointing?

A puppy is never too young to be taken into the fields and woods to build his enjoyment in going with you in search of game and awakening his urge to find it. In little puppies these runs should be brief, only a few minutes at a time. They tire quickly, and you should avoid tiring them until the fun is gone and they lose interest. As the puppy grows older and stronger the workouts can be lengthened.

If in the limited time available you can get your puppy into an area with plentiful wild birds, his birdiness and pointing instinct will develop naturally. Wild birds are great for puppies. They encourage pointing because the puppy soon learns that he cannot get too close to them, and they are also excellent because he cannot catch them.

For lack of wild birds, strong flying quail can be used, but you should first get your puppy accustomed to working on a 30-ft. check-cord. You will have to work him on the check-cord to prevent his catching quail after their short flights.

There is a quicker way to get your puppy birdy and pointing which is very effective. As with quail, this method requires that the puppy be previously trained to range within the limits of the check-cord.

Get three good pigeons, some kite string, three plastic soft-drink bottles and pigeon harnesses for the birds. Now cut three pieces of kite string 40 to 50 feet long. Tie one end of each string to a harnessed pigeon and the other end to a soft-drink bottle. In lieu of pigeon harness you can shackle the bird's legs with a piece of string four or five inches long with a slip knot at either end. Pull the slip knot snug on each of the pigeon's lower legs, and attach your long kite-string in the middle of the shackle. However, I urge the harness as less tiring to the birds.

Put a pigeon down asleep in a birdy area with its soft-drink bottle close by. Set out the other pigeons about 150 feet apart in

A young setter learns about birds and pointing with the aid of a pigeon on a string. Kite string tied to a soft-drink bottle will bring the pigeon gracefully to earth in a short distance to be worked on again.

the same way. If one of the pigeons wakes up prematurely, the bottle will bring it down easily and gracefully at the end of its string.

Now bring on your dog, with the training cord attached to his regular collar or a slip collar. Keep hold of the rope, and work your dog, into the wind for good scenting conditions, toward one of the pigeons. If the dog fails to scent the bird or shows no sign of pointing, don't despair. With your foot (or better yet have a helper do it) nudge the bird to flight. But be very careful that your dog does not get so close to the bird that its flapping wings will hit him in the face and frighten him.

Take your dog in the general direction of the pigeon's flight, again bringing your dog up to the bird facing the wind. This time the bird will be awake, probably standing, and the chances are that your dog will rush forward to catch it. Pull up on the training cord to prevent this, and the dog will freeze into point momentarily. Put the pigeon to flight again, and then move on to the other pigeons, repeating the procedure for each. Then start around again, making each pigeon fly twice this time also. Twice around the field, with two flights for each bird each round, is enough for any dog.

It goes without saying that you shouldn't be stupid enough to leave the check-cord so loose that your dog can catch a pigeon. When your dog points, stroke his belly. If this is the first time your dog has had this treatment, he may lie down or turn his head. Don't be concerned. Don't try to make the dog stand up; a little experience will accustom him to your hands on his body. Go ahead and flush, or have a helper flush, the pigeon.

If you are lucky enough to be working with homing pigeons and have a helper, on the final find with each bird ask your helper to unshackle the pigeon and let it fly home. Let the puppy chase. It will whet his enthusiasm.

If you do not have homers and want to save the birds for another workout on another day, put your dog away while you pick up the pigeons and their gear. Then let the puppy scamper the field, scenting where the pigeons were.

Pigeons tire quickly. If more than one or two dogs are to be trained in one session, there should be replacements for the birds.

Don't shoot over your dog in this type of workout. There is time for that later on. Also don't be concerned in this stage of training on birds if your puppy's points are only fleeting.

What you are doing is awakening your dog's instincts. Once it is clear that the dog is beginning to point, or even just to scent the pigeons with a strong desire to hunt, you have accomplished your purpose. One such workout may be all you need to do this. If more than one session with pigeons on a string is necessary, work your dog elsewhere in between to discourage formation of the habit of puttering in search of heavy scent.

Once your dog has become birdy, don't go back to this lesson. Work him on wild birds whenever you can. But however you have developed your dog's birdiness, don't try to make him staunch or steady at this stage. *Postpone training for staunchness and steadiness until after you have him thoroughly yard trained.* You will never regret it.

How Can I Get My Dog to Work Close on Birds?

This is something that can be taught to a puppy as soon as he learns to love birds, and is valuable training for a bird dog of any age.

Take your dog to an area where you know there is a bird and you have a good location on it, either because you set it out or saw it come down.

As you near the bird order "Close" and begin to whistle in continuing chirps, something like a hen quail chirping. Do it with your lips or make a similar continuing, distinctive noise on your training whistle. Repeat the command "Close" as needed and keep up the chirping whistle until the dog finds the bird. Only a few such experiences and your dog will know the meaning of the command "Close" and that continuing, distinctive whistle.

Do this whenever you are working on a bird in training, and you will have a dog that will add to your hunting pleasure later on. At the command "Close" he will thoroughly work out a birdy area, even though no bird may be found. The command will also help you when you have shot down a bird and are having trouble finding it.

The command has another use when your puppy that has learned to love to hunt is temporarily overcome by his desire for companionship with another dog. If he has learned what the "Close" signal means, you can use it to remind him of what he is missing. Once he has broken away from the other dog you can send him on and usually he will forget all about trailing. But be careful about using the signal this way on a puppy too many times without bird finds in between, or you may find yourself in the boat with the boy who cried wolf when there was none.

3

Elementary Education

What's the Importance of Yard Training?

The period of yard training is a most important time in a dog's development. It is the time in which a bundle of puppy animation and energy begins to become a disciplined member of pointing dog society.

It is also a time when the dog is very impressionable. It is the time for you to analyze your dog carefully to determine whether he is an extrovert or an introvert and how much pressure you can safely apply to achieve the desired results.

The rudiments of yard training are easy to understand, but harder to accomplish with your dog. Yard training is boring, but you must steel yourself to patience and tact. Indelible impressions can be made that will affect all future training.

If you are patient until the dog thoroughly understands each lesson and your wants, you will benefit. In later lessons the dog will accept with alacrity the training needed to build his character without losing his confidence in you. Also, when more restraint and stronger discipline are required later on, the dog will understand that any discipline administered did not result from the bird out there, but simply from his failure to obey your commands.

How Do I Yard Train My Dog?

If you got your puppy while it was very young, and have worked with it as previously suggested, you may feel that you have come a long way on yard training. The methods outlined below are for a puppy 12 to 18, or even 20 months of age. When your puppy gets to this age, follow the schedule outlined below. His earlier training will make the task easier for you, and will cut down on the time required to produce a fully yard trained dog. But you can't give a very young puppy the repetition, repetition, repetition that is needed for solid, lasting yard training; very young puppies tire too quickly.

LESSON 1

This lesson assumes that the dog, having reached 12 months of age, will walk with the leash attached, regardless of its manners. The purpose of the lesson is to teach the dog to heel quietly by your side and to stop there in his tracks when you say "Whoa".

Attach a 30-foot training cord. Don't snap it to the collar, but use the snap to make a slip knot, and put the loop over the dog's head. When the dog pulls, the noose will tighten. When the dog stops pulling, the noose will relax, but it won't fall off if the dog lowers his head.

Let the dog run around dragging the cord for a few minutes, to investigate, urinate, or what not. If it is a dog that has demonstrated that he will be a companion, drop the cord and let the dog run free. If you are afraid that the dog will run off, hold on to the cord until the dog's enthusiasm begins to subside.

Now the lesson starts. Slide one hand along the cord until it is the length of a normal walking leash. In your other hand carry the hollow cardboard tube from a roll of paper towels.

Start walking. The dog pulls you. Go about 30 feet, say "Whoa" and stop. The dog will have to stop, but will mill around. Immediately say "Heel" and pull the dog back to heeling position. Walk another 30 feet and repeat the process.

Your dog will probably give you a hard time. He doesn't understand your wishes. But keep repeating until the dog shows

A puppy gets an early heeling lesson on a check-cord and later heels confidently and happily off leash. Paul with Seth Pope's Carolina Star.

signs of resigning himself to the circumstances by not pulling so hard. Repeat 50 times if necessary.

So far you have been training by persuasion and repetition. Now you are about to introduce a new factor—the discipline that follows when your commands are not obeyed.

Command "Heel" and move forward. If the dog pulls, bop the side of his head with the cardboard tube. The tube can't hurt the dog, but the noise of the tube will be like a percussion cap, and will bring him to attention. Say "Heel" harshly and move forward. Give a good jerk on the cord if the dog rears to the side. Repeat your Heel and Whoa exercise every 30 feet, bopping the dog if it refuses to heel. Three to five bops will usually bring results, even in hard cases.

If your dog rears *backward* at any time, say "Whoa" and let him catch his wits momentarily. Then say "Heel", with a short, hard jerk forward. Invariably, the dog will rush forward. If he stops of his own accord, be ahead of him mentally; command "Whoa" first and then "Heel" to resume the exercise.

When the dog does right, show your appreciation. Petting is

as important a tool as any in your training kit. It is better to pet too much than to jerk too much.

I mentioned three to five bops on the head. Most dogs take less. Whatever the number of bops required to bring your dog into line, repeat the "Whoa" and "Heel" up to 100 times afterward, every thirty feet or so, before you put him up for the day. Then repeat the next time you take him out, the next day, if possible.

You may think I am asking you to repeat the exercises in these lessons too many times (I said yard training was boring, didn't I?). But what you are doing with all that repetition is building a habit pattern in your dog—to obey your commands instantly and automatically. You can call it "brain washing" if you want to, but whatever you call it, the hard work you put into this repetition will save you headaches later on.

Many people carry on their training too long at one time. A dog has a brain the size of a golf ball, and mental exercise tires him quickly. A tired dog, like a tired person, gets obstinate. But a dog will take 150 Whoas every thirty feet without getting obstinate.

One word of caution: the dog that rears backward and refuses to lead almost invariably is an introvert. So modify your discipline accordingly.

When you take your dog out for the second session, follow the same procedure as in the first. No doubt when the training begins your dog will be frisky and cut up. Give him a few minutes to settle down. If necessary to bop him once or twice, do so, but don't be generous with the bops. Repeat the Heel and Whoa exercise 150 times, and then put your dog up.

These first two sessions will tell you whether you have a dog that will quickly fall into line, or one that will challenge you.

LESSON 2

Go on to this lesson only after you are thoroughly sure that your dog understands "Heel" and "Whoa". Let go of the leash and see if the dog will heel and whoa satisfactorily with the cord dragging on the ground. It is really important to brainwash him to heel and whoa so that he obeys these commands easily, naturally, and

Training a dog to hold on "whoa." Testing the dog's ability to hold on "whoa," handler first steps to one side.

with good nature. If not quite sure, review the previous lesson.

If you are sure, you are ready for Lesson 2. Start by heeling and whoaing your dog every 30 feet for about 50 whoas, which will take about five minutes.

Now whoa your dog and step to the *side*, abreast of the dog, about two feet, no more. The dog will start to follow you. Command "Whoa" again. It ought to stop him, but it won't. On this new lesson, the dog can't understand why you want to get away from him.

Quickly step back to the dog, command "Heel" and move on 30 feet. Whoa the dog again and step to the side, as before, the same distance. If he attempts to follow, repeat "Whoa", raising your hand slightly. If the dog does it halfway right, give him praise and petting. If on the other hand he starts to come to you, step to him quickly and put him firmly back in place. If the dog shows nervousness or is upset by your reprimand, go back to the Lesson 1 exercise and heel and whoa him about ten times. Then try the second lesson again and study the reaction.

It may take several evenings, or workouts, to master this lesson. But if, after you have been reasonable and you feel that he really understands, he still comes to you after being whoaed, do this. Gather up the leash, put the dog back in place and bop him with the cardboard tube. Stand by the dog's side until he regains his composure. Then step back again. If the dog insists on following, set him back, repeat "whoa" and bop him again. Several such corrections will make him a believer.

Once you are successful, repeat your heeling, whoaing and stepping back a few times, and put the dog away. Try to stop at a time when the dog has done it correctly, and then praise him no end. But do not let the dog get rambunctious.

Repeat this lesson daily, backing a little farther away each time, until you can step back ten feet from the dog's side without his moving. Keep on repeating until, from ten feet away from his side, you can walk ten feet to his rear and back to him without the dog making a move until you order "Heel".

When your dog meets these requirements, you are on the brink of success, and ready to move on to the next lesson.

LESSON 3

Start by spending a few minutes on the Lesson 1 drill, then on Lesson 2, to remind the dog of what he has learned so far. In all your yard training, start every training session with a review of past learning. It ingrains the habit of doing well the things he knows how to do, promptly and cheerfully, and prepares him to accept the new situation or instructions to come.

Now, after heeling and whoaing, you move out five feet, not directly to the side, but at a 45-degree angle to the front. Why not directly in front? If you step directly in front, you are like a

After the dog has passed that test, handler moves out at an angle.

magnet to the dog. By stepping out at a 45-degree angle, you are asking him to do only a little more than he has done before. Use the same procedures as in Lesson 2 until results are achieved.

Once the results are satisfactory in this situation, spend about five minutes reviewing Lessons 1 & 2 and this lesson so far. Then instead of walking out at an angle, walk out five feet directly ahead of the dog. The chances are good that he will stay in place. If he doesn't, use the same procedures.

Repetitive drill is all that is needed to make your dog stand at the command "Whoa", no matter where you move. Until he will stand without moving, whether you go three, five, or a hundred feet forward, sideward, or backward, he does not understand his teaching. *You* have failed, not the dog. Go back to the lessons you failed on. Don't lose your temper. It's easy to say, "I'll show that damn dog!" Don't "show" him; teach him.

LESSON 4

Up to this point, you have taught your dog to heel quietly by your side with the checkcord dragging; to stop in his tracks at the command of "Whoa", and having stopped, to stay where he is without moving, or unpleasantness will follow, while you walk any reasonable distance in any direction.

Now you are ready to teach your dog to come to you when you call "Here" or his name, and to stop at any given point when you command "Whoa".

Start by reviewing Lessons 1, 2 & 3 for a few minutes.

Then heel your dog for a few feet and whoa him. Command him to stay, and walk the checkcord out until you are about 30 feet in front of the dog. You have taught the dog to stay where whoaed, and he must do so now.

Standing 30 feet in front of the dog, signal him to come to you by whatever means you prefer—"Here", "Come", his name, or a whistle signal. Since he has been taught to stay where whoaed, he will probably hesitate. If so, give the cord a light pull, repeating your command, and pet the dog when he comes. Move on and repeat this procedure 100 times, making sure that the dog stays where whoaed until ordered to come. Then put your dog away for the day.

Handler commands dog to stay and moves
directly in front of him.

Standing in front of the dog,
signal him to come.

Probably, after a few "Heres", the dog will anticipate the command, and break before you give it. If so, shorten your distance to 15 feet. Then when he breaks before command, set him back firmly, repeating "Whoa". If after three setbacks, he persists in breaking, bop him with the cardboard tube. After a couple of setbacks with bops, most dogs get the message.

Once you have your dog staying in place until called to come, you are ready for the next step. That is to start him with a "Here" and stop him en route with a "Whoa".

Start this not more than 15 feet from the dog. Command "Here" and whoa him as soon as he comes about three feet. Don't let the dog come too far before you whoa him, or his momentum will carry him to you. Your command may slow him down, but it won't stop him. So give the dog a break by not asking too much of him at first.

When, after heeling and whoaing your dog, you can move out 15 feet, start him coming toward you with a "Here" and stop him as soon as he has come two or three feet with another "Whoa", you are ready to vary your procedure. Now, after heeling and whoaing, don't move out so far. Move out only about 8 feet. Call the dog to you and stop him halfway with a whoa. Repeat this a hundred times, heeling the dog 30 feet or so between repetitions. After this, begin moving out farther before you call the dog, until eventually you can move 30 to 50 feet out and can start and stop the dog several times before he reaches you.

Keep in mind that this is a confusing lesson for the dog. He will stop at "Whoa" and be reluctant to come when called for fear of a reprimand. Give the dog confidence by petting and praising him warmly when he responds correctly. Don't expect perfection too soon, and don't reprimand the dog when he takes only a step or two when commanded to whoa.

Dogs tire quickly on this lesson. You are giving two opposing commands, and this is hard on them mentally. Don't crowd too much of the lesson in one training session. Take it in bites, and quit before the dog gets tired and obstinate. But, and I can't emphasize this too much, always start any training session with a review of what the dog has learned to do well. Try to quit at a time when the dog is doing well on the new instructions. Then have him repeat the new accomplishments a few more times. Show gratitude and paise him warmly; then put the dog up for the day.

Of the two commands you are working on, "Whoa" is the more important; you can always walk to a dog that stays where commanded. But you won't have to if you train on the "Here" command only enough to insure that your dog will come to you when called.

LESSON 5

Your dog is now heeling, whoaing anywhere you command it to stop, and coming to you when called. You have been working all this time with a checkcord attached to the dog, and you should continue to do so. The dog's education is just beginning.

The time has come to teach the dog to stay without moving where whoaed as you pick up or kick up objects in front of him. Now is the time to teach this, not when your dog is pointing live game.

As always, start by "brainwashing" your dog on previous lessons. Then after heeling for about 30 feet, whoa him, look for some small object on the ground, and reach down for it. The dog

To test his dog, the handler commands "whoa" and pretends to search for an object on the ground.

will lean forward, or step forward, to help you. Command "Whoa".

If the dog disobeys, give him the benefit of the doubt. Heel him on another 30 feet. Order "Whoa" and "Stay", and reach down for another object. If the dog moves to help you, command "Whoa" harshly and set him back in his original position. Then finish picking up the object. Repeat heeling 30 feet, whoaing and picking up object, setting the dog back when necessary, until you are satisfied that you can go through this procedure without your dog moving.

Most dogs, whether extroverts or introverts, catch on to this part of the lesson readily. Why? They have previously been thoroughly drilled in what "Whoa" means. The only thing you have to overcome here is their interest in your movement.

Now make the training a little more difficult, and your dog's obedience more certain when live game is introduced. Have your wife, your girlfriend, or the cook at your favorite restaurant, bake a pound of liver as hard as a rock. Cut the liver into fudge-size squares for your next workout.

In this session, after you have heeled your dog and commanded "Whoa" and "Stay", walk out a few feet and drop the liver in front of the dog. The scent will entice him to move. If he does, command "Whoa" and pick up the liver. If he insists on moving, set him back, as in earlier sessions, repeating the command to whoa. If a few such setbacks don't do the trick, you should know by now how to use the cardboard tube, but probably you won't have to. When the dog does well, reward him occasionally with a piece of the liver and pet him.

Don't throw the liver on the ground where you are going to heel him. The dog will start to hunt the liver, and you don't want this. Drop the liver only two or three feet in front of the dog each time you whoa him. And don't try to show off, or test your dog unduly at this point, by throwing the liver out ahead of him, and trying to stop him with a "Whoa" en route to the liver. This is not the time, and nothing will be gained.

When you and your dog have completed all of these lessons satisfactorily, his yard training is done. In fact, you have your dog about 80 percent completely trained.

You have your dog under control. He has thoroughly learned the essential commands, and also thoroughly learned that failure to obey your commands results in unpleasantness.

He has learned that this unpleasantness is due entirely to his disobedience, not to anything else in his situation at the moment. A dog so trained will not become a blinker; that is, a dog that avoids birds when scented to avoid unpleasant consequences. Later when your dog breaks commands while on a bird, he will not associate his punishment with the bird, but with his act of disobedience.

A dog not so thoroughly yard-broken can easily be made into a blinker in later training. Not being thoroughly trained to obey, he requires more and stronger discipline. He comes to associate his punishment with the bird. His instincts compel him to hunt for birds, but when he gets hot scent, he backs off, circles, or runs away, to avoid the pain he has come to link with that scent. That is his escape hatch.

What About a Dog That Sits or Drops in Yard Training?

Sitting or dropping when given other commands usually indicates a timid, introverted dog. He can know what you mean and still do this. It is one more form of escape hatch, and adds to your burdens as a trainer.

If your dog starts this, lighten your discipline and slow down your training. In other words, be gentle and take it easy. Let the dog get to enjoy what he does before you move on to something more difficult.

There is, however, something more you can do about it, another variation of the Heel & Whoa routine. Don't try to get the dog to stand by jerking the leash or lifting him up, and avoid all bopping. When he starts to sit, say "Whoa" immediately followed by "Heel". It keeps the dog off balance, gives him a sense of urgency and no time to decide to sit or drop. He soon decides it is easier to stand. You, however, must be one jump ahead of the dog mentally, anticipate his plans, and thwart them before he can carry them out. A number of lessons in an easy-going manner, in which nothing else is required of the dog, will get across the idea that you want him to stand.

It is a correctable fault. Ignoring it with the hope that in time it will go away will just accentuate it.

Why Can't I Use an Electronic Trainer in Yard Training?

You can, but I recommend it only as a last resort.

It is possible to teach heeling and whoaing entirely with the electronic trainer, but I do not recommend it to the inexperienced. The electronic trainer is a great servant when properly used, but it is a poor master in the hands of a neophyte trainer working with a dog not yet indoctrinated to discipline. Inexpert use can be very upsetting to a dog, whereas very few dogs are upset by traditional methods of yard training. In traditional training, correction is made significant to the dog as much by the tone of your voice as by any discomfort administered.

However, suppose that your dog insists on pulling on the leash, no matter how many times you have repeated the lesson in heeling. Some dogs, usually extroverts, just don't want to quit pulling when supposedly heeling. Try a spiked training collar. Don't let the dog keep up a steady pull against a collar of this type. Say "Heel" and give a strong jerk, adjusting the strength of the jerk to the hardheadedness of the dog. If the first try makes little impression, repeat the command "Heel", jerking harder and sharper.

Pulling has been conquered by this method for years, but if it fails you, try the electronic collar. Put the collar on the dog and command him to heel. If he fails to do so, shock him. It will upset the dog. Let the impression sink in for a while. Then order "Heel" again, and if necessary shock the dog again. Use discretion. By now you should know your dog and how much is enough. If the dog pulls back, refusing to follow, pet him first, and then order "Heel" and give him another light shock.

A dog like this may also be giving you trouble on the "Whoa" command. You have got him heeling properly and are ready to use the trainer to get him to whoa. Order the dog to heel, and as he is walking meekly by your side command "Whoa" and give him a light shock, stopping as you give the command. Then heel the dog a ways and repeat, shocking the dog again if necessary. Give the dog the benefit of the doubt; any semblance of obedience to the command "Whoa" is sufficient. As in all lessons, praise and pet the dog when he does well. Make the session short and use the electronic trainer sparingly, no more than you have to.

The electronic trainer has proved your point: your commands must be obeyed. Revert to the traditional methods outlined in the Yard Training lessons as soon as you can, and follow the procedures I have recommended in these lessons. Hold your electronic trainer in reserve for use only if and when milder forms of discipline prove ineffective with your dog.

But never in yard training attempt to whoa your dog from a distance with an electronic trainer. He won't stop in his tracks, as you had hoped. He will come running to you for sympathy, or, if not too sure of you, may bolt off to your car or the kennel. If you get your dog running to you at the command "Whoa", you are in real trouble. Only fear of you resulting from drastic punishment will stop it.

How Should I Introduce the Gun?

If you have a young puppy and want to start getting it used to loud noises early in life, get a cap pistol and a blank pistol that shoots the foreign made crimps—regular American .22 blanks make too loud a crack.

Wait until your puppy has been introduced to the fields and has found something chasable. When he is going away and no longer near you, fire the cap pistol. If the puppy shows fear or any abnormal reaction, put the pistol away for the day. Go on hunting for something else that the puppy will have fun chasing. But don't make any kind of a fuss over him. That is the worst thing you can do with a dog of any age that shows a sign of gunshyness; it will only accentuate the trait.

Chances are that the puppy will be so much interested in chasing the meadowlark or whatever that he will pay no attention to the noise of the pistol, and after a few repetitions will associate it with a lot of fun.

However if the puppy did show signs of being upset, wait until he is older and more interested in hunting before you try it again.

Once the puppy has grown accustomed to the cap pistol, substitute the blank pistol under the same conditions. Next, I favor a .22 loaded with rat shot, which makes a noise dogs seem to like. Then move up to a shotgun, preferably a .410 before using a heavier gauge, although with most puppies by this time it will make no difference.

With an older dog you can follow the same general procedure, but if he is past the stage where chippie birds interest him, you may have to look longer for something chasable. If game is scarce and you have a quail pen, use your quail. If you don't have quail look for a pigeon fancier in your neighborhood from whom you can rent a few birds; his loss will be negligible because the birds will return to his loft.

If you use pigeons, carry a few in the game bag of your hunting coat. As your dog is running the fields and comes by you, toss a pigeon out and let him have a lusty chase. Throw the bird underhand. For some strange reason, dogs seldom see birds thrown overhand. Repeat this several times until your dog is coming back to you, looking for you to throw another bird. Now is the time to shoot, on the next chase. Whatever the dog's reaction, don't overdo it. One shot is enough for the first workout.

If you have both pigeons and quail to work with, you can do something more than just indoctrinate your dog to the gun. After your dog has become enthusiastic about chasing pigeons, take along a couple of pigeons and a couple of Bobwhite quail on your next workout. Hobble each quail by tying its legs together to insure short flight.

Have a 30-ft. check-cord on your dog, letting him drag it as he runs. Toss a pigeon ahead of the dog and let him have a good chase. When the dog returns for another excursion, have a Bobwhite ready. Throw it underhand high in the air. It will come down in a short distance and your dog will get to it quickly. Be prepared. As the dog picks up the bird, grab the rope and entice the dog to you. The excited puppy won't know what to do with the bird. Having the check-cord, you can coax the dog to you and take the bird from his mouth. If the pup doesn't want to let go, blow in his ear. So far you have used no gun, but the puppy has been indoctrinated in the whole picture of what is expected of him except for the gun's bang.

Now you are ready to introduce the gun. I recommend beginning with crimped blanks and then moving up to .22 rat shot or a .410 as the dog demonstrates lack of concern. Let him chase another pigeon first. Then be prepared to shoot when you follow up by throwing up a quail. Again throw it underhand high in the air. When the bird reaches the height at which you would shoot and starts to fall, fire your gun. By this time the dog will be trying to pick up the bird. Grab the cord and coax the dog to you, blowing in his ear if necessary to make him release the bird. Repeat this procedure in three more workouts and your dog will be conditioned to the gun. But until you are sure that the noise is only incidental to the dog, shoot only once in each workout. When it becomes obvious that the noise does not bother him, you can shoot more times.

This method does not weaken the dog's pointing instinct, nor encourage him to jump in on game. Whatever he does, he is not doing wrong as you have not yet trained him otherwise. The method can be used either before or after you have got your dog birdy and pointing, by the pigeon-on-a-string method or by other means. Obviously of course it should *never* be used after you have begun training for staunchness and steadiness.

It is very important that by one means or another you accustom your dog to gunfire before you take him hunting or begin any aspect of training that requires shooting.

Thoughtless shooting over young dogs before they have learned to accept the bang as part of the fun of hunting is the principal cause of gunshyness. It is hard to believe that such things are done, but they are. A young dog with little or no field experience is taken out because hunting season has begun. While the dog is milling around finding out what it is all about, three magnum loads are fired nearby in quick succession. The only surer way to make a dog gunshy is to take him to a skeetshoot and let the skeetshooters do the job for you.

A dog's ear is sensitive to the sharp, hard crack of a gun, particularly to blanks of American make and shotgun loads. It is much more unpleasant to a dog's ears than to yours. In fact it is reaction to this noise that makes some dogs sit or drop at shot, even though they are not gunshy. But very few dogs become gunshy if they are introduced to the bang while they are overcome with the delight of chasing game, particularly if the trainer begins with a light noise and works up to louder noises in easy stages.

4

Higher Learning

How Should a Dog Be Conditioned before Training on Birds?

He should be thoroughly yard trained, especially to the "Whoa" command. He should be conditioned to the gun and also to running with a check-cord dragging. He should be so accustomed to the check-cord that when he encounters game and you pick up the cord, he will continue to work freely. If not, the combined experience of winding a bird and the restraint of the cord will be upsetting to the dog, and the results will be aggravating to you.

What Birds Should I Liberate for Training?

With the right methods, you could train your dog on any bird that gives off scent and flies. There was, in fact, a time when trainers used guinea fowl. The birds commonly used today are Bobwhite quail, Coturnix quail, pigeons and pheasants. Some have special advantages at certain stages of training, but you will probably have to take into consideration their availability, your situation for housing birds, and cost.

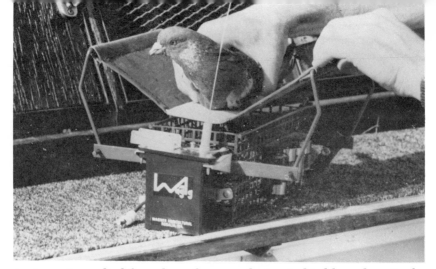

A pigeon is readied for release from an electronic bird launcher. Such devices give the trainer precise timing in releasing the bird, coupled with the freedom to handle the dog in a controlled field situation.

PIGEONS

Pigeons are excellent for early training on birds. If you can provide a loft, or cultivate a friend who has one, homing pigeons will fly back to it even when released miles away, and can be used over and over. Common pigeons will also return to their loft if released nearby, but you can't count on it if taken very far. But they are not expensive, and there are times when it will help your dog to shoot one for him.

BOBWHITE QUAIL

Bobwhite quail are used at some stage of training by most professional trainers. They are relatively inexpensive, and if you have a covey holder, they too can be used repeatedly.

In some states it is illegal to recapture quail. Check with your Conservation Department, and find out also if you need a license. The license will not be expensive. Your Conservation Department may be able to give you a list of breeders within the state from whom you can buy birds.

If you have land of your own, or know a landowner who will let you use his, make or buy a covey holder. There are almost as many designs for covey holders as there are fellows who build them. The fact is that, when in a coveying mood, liberated Bob-

A pair of bobwhite quail (cock bird on right).

white quail will return to, and try to enter, anything sheltering the rest of the covey. Basically, you need a wire pen big enough to accommodate about 15 quail, with a shelter of exterior plywood or similar material on one end and access doors on both ends.

There are advantages in making a pen with two compartments—one as a holding pen and the other for released birds returning to the covey—with some form of a closable opening between the two compartments. The compartments can be either side by side or one above the other. Make your frame of 2-by-2's and cover it all, except the shelter, with 1/2-in. hardware cloth, including the bottom and the separation between the compartments.

The shelter should have a wood floor on which the birds can gather in bad weather or on cold nights, and the side toward the wire should also be solid except for an opening about 4 inches high across the bottom.

For sanitary reasons, the pen should be raised a little off the ground, unless you plan to move it to fresh ground frequently. If raised, and the ground is irregular, you will need to close off any gaps made by low ground that are big enough to let returning birds get under, rather than into, the pen.

A two-compartment pen gives some protection against rats, weasels, or other predators that can come in through recall openings. The predators will not be able to get at the birds in the holding compartment. Also, if you use adult quail, you will need to separate the sexes during the mating season, keeping the fe-

A good two compartment covey holder built by amateur trainer George Gladd. To fly birds out, door at left is opened.

males in the holding pen and releasing only males. During mating season, adults are likely to pair off and nest outside.

Make a small sliding release door in any compartment from which you plan to release birds, and make one or two entrances in your recall compartment for returning birds. An entrance is made by forming a slightly conical tube of hardware cloth, about 9 inches long, 3 inches in diameter at the small end and 4 inches at the large end. Trim the large end of the tube so that when mounted on vertical wire it will cant upward at a 45-degree angle. Mount it at the bottom of some side, projecting into the pen. Sew the tube in place with wire to strengthen it against marauders, and cut the opening in the side wire. If your pen is raised slightly above ground, make a ramp of some sort up to the entrance. A ramp that is hinged to the bottom rail of the pen has another advantage. It can be raised to close the recall funnel as a safeguard against predators when you have no quail outside the pen.

The size of your compartments will depend on the number of birds you plan to keep. A wire compartment 5 ft. long by 2½ ft. wide is ample for 15 quail. Height is not critical; 18 inches will do.

Although many pens are used without this protection, it is a good idea to put a 4 ft. fence all around your pen to fend off stray dogs and other large marauders. If the fence wire is small mesh, make a few openings at the bottom big enough for quail to enter.

To release birds you need only open the release door and shoo a few out, or you can put a small cage in front of the door and shoo in some that you can spot where you please.

Even if your state bans recapture, you can benefit from a covey holder. And a one-compartment pen with no recall funnels will do. After a few days to let the birds come to feel at home in their pen, let a few out and scatter grain around the pen. As long as they can get food, they will stay nearby. With several such covey holders, you can have a virtual game preserve with several semi-wild coveys.

For your covey holder you will of course need a food hopper and water dish, plus fine sand for dusting, chick grit and feed. Small scratch grain will do for feed, but game-bird-and-turkey pellets provide a better diet. Small feed hoppers filled from ouside the pen and inexpensive water containers are available from the big mail-order houses, if you don't find them locally. A box will do for the sand, and the grit can be mixed in or supplied separately. If your hopper feeds from outside, devise some method of securing the lid against raccoons, which will soon find out how to open it.

So now you have a covey holder. If you are buying young birds, try to get them about eight weeks old. Don't work your dog on them immediately. After a couple of days in the pen, let several out around the pen, preferably in early evening, and leave them undisturbed. By nightfall, they will probably have found their way back in.

Do this several times over a week or so, and then you can begin working your dog on them. Don't let a lot out at one time. They may form a new covey outside the pen. And try not to work the same bird more than twice in any outing. You may drive it so far from the pen that it won't return.

An ideal spot for a covey holder is where your dog can work on all sides of it, and the birds won't fly to a thick hedgerow or other impenetrable cover on the first flush. A close-by hedgerow is great for birds working their way home, but you will find it difficult to flush out birds that fly to it. However, ground cover should preferably be enough so that birds coming back will not be in open view to hawks. They are quick to spot hawks and will dart to any nearby clumps that will hide them.

In buying Bobwhite quail, try to get all you will need from the same place at the same time. If more are added later, the new birds and the old ones will fight. Even if they don't kill each other, birds released may decide that life outside the pen is better. Put new birds in a separate covey holder if you can. If you can't, at least put all your old birds in one compartment and the new birds in the other. They will fight through the wire, but the damage won't be serious. After a week or so of getting acquainted, you may be able to let them intermingle.

If your birds pick each other for other reasons, some greenery in the pen—alfalfa, clover, or the like—may help.

Birds from 10 to 14 weeks old return best to the pen. Most will continue to return after that, but hens that are beginning to lay sometimes stay out. Quail stand the cold well, and can be wintered over, even in northern States, if kept supplied with food, grit, sand, and snow as a substitute for water. But come late April, you had better separate them and let only one sex out—I recommend the males—if you want them to come back.

COTURNIX QUAIL

If you have only a limited area to work your dog in, no covey holder or pigeon loft, and expense is a major factor, you may want to seek out a breeder of Coturnix quail. These little birds are often called Japanese quail although they are, in truth, the quail of the Holy Land mentioned in the Old Testament. They are generally less expensive than Bobwhite quail, and their advantages for you may outweigh their disadvantages.

They do not covey, but are easy to pick up after a workout. They are tough and hardy and can be used over and over for months. A relatively small wooden box with a wire top and bottom will house them happily if kept where they will get the benefit of the sun but it is not too hot. They will thrive on scratch grain, with of course some sand, grit and water.

Except in the mating season, they throw off strong scent, and dogs love to point them, even dogs that have a tendency to blink or circle. They stay put where set down or when coming to a stop after flight. They are so tame that they can easily be picked up to throw in the air for a flush or take back to the pen after a workout. On the other hand, their tameness makes them easy prey to dogs not under control, and requires extra care on the part of the handler.

Coturnix (or Japanese) quail.

Like all game birds, when flushed they will fly with the wind if they can. With the wind, they may fly up to 300 feet, but more often about a hundred feet. If forced into the wind, they may flop to the ground. Their behavior is not predictable. Sometimes they will flush wild at slight provocation and moments later crouch and refuse to budge.

Coturnix prefer open fields with sparse cover. In one way, this is good, because they are hard to see on the ground. Their markings provide good camouflage, which they enhance by burrowing into the grass. If forced into heavy cover, it is next to impossible to get a good point on them or to see them. Difficulties in heavy cover are increased by their trait, when landing from flight, of running perhaps up to 30 feet, leaving bewildering scent for a dog.

A bad feature of their preference for open, light cover is that this does not encourage a dog to range to the objectives where native gamebirds are more likely to be found.

Coturnix are very prolific. In warm weather, hens will begin laying an egg a day at ten weeks of age, and when laying they seem to give off little or no scent.

The difficulty of seeing them on the ground is easily overcome by attaching about eight inches of bright string, white or yellow, to each bird before release. When your dog points, or at the end of a workout, you look for the string. Their lack of fear makes it easy to lean down and pick them up.

With all their faults, they are a useful little bird, especially in the colder months. Rarely moving when set out, they are excellent for teaching staunchness when precautions are taken against their being caught by the dog. There will, however, come a time in later training when you will need to work your dog on Bobwhite or other native birds. Although they love to point them, dogs do tire of Coturnix in time. Then you will want to switch to other birds to kindle your dog's enthusiasm for hunting and ranging.

PHEASANTS

Pheasants are excellent. Their drawback is expense. If it were not for that, many more of them would be used in training. Full-grown birds are costly, and not many of the people who want to train their dogs can provide the facilities needed to raise a flock.

However, unless you live in country where your dog will never encounter a pheasant, you should try to use a few, at least in late training. Many a dog that has seemed rock solid on quail has come unstrung when challenged by the noisy take-off of a big pheasant.

In some States where the shooting of hens is prohibited, State game farms are breeding a strain of pheasants in which all hens are blonde, while cocks have the typical coloration of ring-necks. The sex of chicks is evident when they emerge from their shells.

Cock pheasant: excellent, although expensive, birds for training.

This enables the game farms to rear cocks to release for hunting, and to dispose of surplus female chicks.

Surplus chicks are sold at a low price. This makes it possible for a person with a brooder to raise the chicks until they are old enough to handle themselves in the wild, when they can be used in training. The same thing could of course be done with chicks from other sources, but the cost would undoubtedly be higher.

If you are lucky enough to be so situated that you can have the large pen, high enough for a man to walk in, that grown pheasants require, you would benefit from one. Pheasants are not a covey bird, but it is quite common to see birds that have lived in a well-located pen for some time walking around the pen, trying to get in, a day or so after release. If there is a funnel of sufficient size similar to the funnel of a quail pen, they will enter. But a funnel big enough to admit a pheasant will also let in sizable predators. It should therefore be closed nights and on days when not needed. Pheasants cannot be counted on to return to a pen if driven far off by a second flush, especially if they find there food and cover more to their liking than your land provides.

How Do I Hide a Bird to Work My Dog On?

There are four ways to set and hide birds.

The first is the quail pen. You simply open the release door and flush out a number of birds. They will hide themselves.

The second is used when you want to put a bird down in a known spot, and bring your dog up to it. It will work on pheasants, pigeons or Bobwhite quail, and Coturnix don't need it. Fold the bird's head gently under its right wing. Lay the bird down, with its head and wing to the ground and pointing into the breeze at a 45-degree angle. Look for a spot where the air moves over the bird gently; birds are harder to plant in a strong wind. Keep your index finger on the bird until it makes ever so slight a movement; then withdraw your finger. The bird will usually stay for 20 minutes or more. To avoid sight pointing, a little dead grass can be put over the bird. But don't make it so thick that your dog won't get scent. Have a check-cord on your dog when you use this method. The bird is asleep and at the mercy of an untrained dog.

For young dogs that are liable to jump in after pointing only

Above left: Hiding or planting a bird: prepare a spot for the bird by tunneling in the grass with your toe. Right: Place the bird's head under one wing and lay bird on its side, with head down, in the prepared spot.

Below left: Gently stretch both legs to the rear. Right: Lightly cover the bird with grass.

momentarily, a third method is recommended if you are using quail or pheasants. Put the bird down in its natural position, pressing on its neckbone with your index finger. The bird will open its mouth, give a slight heave, and relax. Then remove your finger. Birds put down this way will also stay for some 20 minutes, but if threatened by an impulsive dog will flush and escape. The method will work with quail or pheasants, but not with pigeons. The pigeon is not a ground bird and will not stay.

A fourth procedure, which will work with pheasants or quail but not with pigeons, puts out a bird that will react most like a bird in the wild. Throw the bird down in cover 18 to 24 inches high. Throw it at an angle slightly less than 45 degrees, not hard enough to injure the bird, but hard enough to knock the wind out of it. When the bird gathers its wits, the high cover will give it the protection it seeks. It will stay in the area, but will be quick to take flight when threatened. It will not be easily caught by an untrained dog, and undo the progress you have made.

I have not mentioned dizzying the bird in any of these methods. Dizzying increases the chances of your dog pouncing on a bird in its bewildered state. People seem to have particular trouble in setting out pigeons, and often end up dizzying the bird to the point where it cannot fly. Yet it is comparatively easy to set out a pigeon, once you have got the knack. Practice putting out birds before you try to work your dog on them. It is better to spend a little time this way than to have the birds flush prematurely when training.

How About an Electronic Collar When Training on Birds?

An electronic trainer will prove invaluable in this stage of your dog's development. It is surprising how few people use the trainer here. The reason may be that they have heard of instances where the wrong approach produced unhappy results.

I cannot say this too many times; never shock your dog when he is pointing game hidden in the cover. A dog on point is under the spell of his instincts. If you shock a dog under these circumstances you associate pointing with pain. Thereafter his pointing instinct may be overpowered by his instinctive reaction to fear. He will leave the point, or, in dog language, blink.

There is no need to take this risk. Properly used, the electronic trainer can do the job without taking anything out of your dog.

How Will My Dog React to the Shock?

Like people, dogs vary in their reactions to discomfort. Most dogs yip and jump a little when the shock hits them. Some, after the first few experiences, only shake their heads a little, as they might for an insect sting.

In their first experience, dogs generally react in one of three ways:

1. Jump and come running to you for sympathy and protection.
2. Bolt and run off.
3. Freeze in their tracks, refusing to bolt or turn or come to you.

Your dog will probably react in one of the first two ways. Whichever it is, when he reaches the point where he will come to you on feeling the sting of the trainer, if he didn't at first, you have the upper hand. He will be amenable to further electronic training. But until your dog is well along in finishing school continue to use a check-cord on him when using the electronic collar. It is especially important to have one—I recommend 50 feet of 3/8-in. nylon—the first time you use the trainer. When the dog has ranged nearly to the end of the chord, give your command, and shock him if necessary. You have two safeguards, the rope to prevent bolting in panic and the electronic trainer to give another shock if needed to bring obedience.

Dogs that react in the third way—that is, freeze in their tracks—are usually difficult to train. They have low IQ's and are bewildered. If your dog freezes, repeat the shock. If he still doesn't move, shock him once more. If, after the third shock, he doesn't come to you or try to bolt, walk to him and pet him. Coax him to move out and resume hunting. When the dog is running normally again, wait for a time when he is only ten or twenty feet away and shock him. If he doesn't react by either coming to you or changing direction, put him in the kennel and leave him there several days.

Sometimes after a layoff dogs of this category will respond to commands with no further shocking, but if you try every day to get them to respond normally they will go backward in their training. When you resume workouts after the layoff, if your dog still freezes, repeat the first day's procedure. If you can get him to run to you for protection, you have won the battle, and you can continue to use your electronic trainer. But if, after all this, the dog continues to freeze when shocked, you had better put aside your electronic training aid. You will need to study your dog and other training methods to decide how you can continue his education without an electronic trainer.

How Powerful a Trainer Do I Need?

Some electronic trainers are advertised as reaching here and there for ungodly distances. Why wait until a dog gets farther out in the woods and fields than you really want him to go? In your training to develop a finished dog why not use a 50-ft. check-cord? Common sense will tell you that if your dog ranges out of ken of your voice and whistle, he is out of control and needs more close-in training. Further, you should never shock a dog that you cannot see. He could be on point.

Electronic trainers with extreme range may be of value to a person training a big-going dog for wide open spaces, but aren't ordinarily needed in training a dog that will be useful in most hunting cover.

How Do I Make My Dog Staunch?

What do you mean by "staunch"? Some people use the terms "staunch" and "steady" interchangeably. For the purposes of this book at least, consider a staunch dog to be one that holds a point until the handler puts the bird to flight. A steady dog is one that continues to stand while the bird is flushed and shot, not moving until heeled away or ordered on.

Since you are ready to make your dog staunch, I am assuming that the dog is now hunting, and loves game and the gun. I am assuming also that he is accustomed to the check-cord, and will run naturally with the cord trailing. You have developed his nose on birds and induced pointing by working him on wild or liberated

Stroking a dog on point induces confidence and tranquillity.

gamebirds or by my pigeon-on-a-string method. You have been stroking him on the belly to induce confidence, and you have thoroughly yard-trained him to understand and obey the command "Whoa". The long hours spent in repetitive drill that you may have considered drudgery getting your dog to obey your commands cheerfully and automatically will pay off here. This is where it all comes into focus.

If wild birds are plentiful in your area, so much the better. You can work in the fields and woods, and your dog will develop naturally with your enforcement of the command "Whoa".

If you use liberated quail, release several some distance apart around your training area. Now bring on your dog, trailing a 30-ft. check-cord. Work him away from the birds until he runs off his initial exuberance. Then gradually swing him until he is headed into the wind toward one of the birds. If your dog has demonstrated to you that his pointing instinct is strong, let the check-cord trail. If you suspect that his point will be only fleeting, hold the cord as you guide him to the bird.

In either case, when the dog scents game and stops or pauses, order "Whoa" firmly but quietly. Holding the dog with the check-cord, walk up the cord with your hands until you can stroke him. Stroke his back and his belly, especially his belly, to induce confidence and tranquility.

If at all possible, have a helper when training for staunchness—your spouse, little boy or girl, or the kid next door will do. The helper's job is to walk ahead when instructed, flush the bird, and fire a blank charge.

Very likely, when your helper walks ahead, your dog will want to go too. Command "Whoa" in a strong, but not excited, tone. If this doesn't stop the dog, bop his ear with a cardboard tube and repeat "Whoa" harshly, halting your helper momentarily while you again stabilize the dog by stroking. Then have your helper flush the bird and fire. If the dog attempts to chase, speak to him and give him a light reprimand. After the bird has flown, heel or collar your dog away and proceed to the next bird.

Bear in mind that in this lesson you are working only to make your dog staunch, and your goal is to do this without taking away any of his natural beauty on point. Here is where your dog can be developed to full potential by patient training, or he can be ruined by excited, perhaps angry, shouting or harsh handling. Do not even consider using the electronic trainer in teaching staunchness. There will be a time for the electronic aid when you move on to making your dog steady to wing and shot by taking the chase out of him.

You really should have a helper when teaching staunchness, especially in your early workouts, but if this is impossible there still is a way. Follow the procedure already outlined, except don't flush the first few birds. Instead, after you have stabilized your dog, pick him up bodily and walk about 40 feet to the rear. Then put him down and proceed to the next bird. Keep a firm grip on the check-cord and insist that the dog go where instructed.

After working in this fashion on six or seven birds, you should be able, after stroking and stabilizing your dog, to walk quietly ahead and flush the bird. But keep your grip on the check-cord, or be ready to grab it. Caution your dog to whoa as you flush the bird, and stop him with the cord if he attempts to chase. Set him firmly back in place, repeating "Whoa", as you did in yard training. Then heel him away and go on to the next bird.

There is yet another variation of training for staunchness that works very well. It has advantages for those whose training area is limited or who have trouble making birds stay put, but here again you need a helper if you can get one.

*Wooden
bird box
with quail.*

Build three wooden boxes, 10 in. by 5 in. by 5 in., big enough
to hold a pigeon, two or three Bobwhites, or half a dozen Coturnix.
Put hinges on the covers and bore holes throughout the covers
and all sides. Any of the birds mentioned can be used in the
boxes, but pigeons are particularly good because they fly away
without landing. They tend to develop a dog that watches the
flight with a high, immovable head, which will please the judges
if you are training for field trials.

Out of the dog's sight, spot the loaded boxes in light cover
around your training area. Then proceed much as you would with
other methods. Work your dog away for a while before heading
upwind toward a box. Handle your dog on point as you would
otherwise. When the dog is stabilized, send your helper in to
throw the bird and shoot.

In working with the boxes, carry your dog away bodily after
the flush of the first few birds. Later, as you develop control, heel
him away before moving to the next bird. For some reason, carrying or heeling the dog away takes away his desire to rush back
and investigate the box that concealed the game.

The box procedure, good at any time of the year, is helpful in
summer in States that ban dogs from the fields during the months
when game is nesting and rearing young. With pigeons it can
even be used in weedy vacant tracts in urban areas. But in summer
look for a day with a good breeze. When it is hot, a bag of crushed
ice will help you. Put a layer of the ice in the bottom of each box
and cover it with a newspaper or layer of sawdust to retard melt-
ing. The birds above the ice will give off great scent.

However you go about developing staunchness in your dog,

three points per workout are usually enough. If you want more, wait half an hour before starting over again.

Whether you work with wild birds, liberated gamebirds, or pigeons in boxes, have a helper if you possibly can. Try to avoid leaving your dog unguarded while you walk ahead to flush and shoot until you are sure you can stop him with a "Whoa" the instant he telegraphs intention to break.

When you have reached the stage where your dog will consistently let you walk in front of him, you are on your way to having a confident, strong-pointing dog which, with a "Whoa" if necessary, will stay on a point once established.

I do not recommend it, if only because it will complicate and prolong this phase of training, but if for some reason your dog was not previously introduced to the gun, it can be done while teaching staunchness.

On the first few birds, carry an unloaded air rifle. As your helper flushes the bird, restrain your dog with one hand and fire the air rifle with the other. An empty air rifle has no bang and makes a sound the dog will enjoy. Then switch to a .22 rifle loaded with rat shot, not a rifle bullet. Rat shot also makes a pleasant sound. After several rounds of rat shot with no noticeable reaction, switch to a .410 shotgun.

Now have your helper carry the shotgun and shoot the bird he flushes. Instruct him to walk out, pick up the bird, and bring it back for the dog to smell. Subsequently have the helper fire the shotgun on all flushes while you work with your dog, and occasionally have him kill a bird and bring it back for the dog to sniff.

How Should I Steady My Dog to Wing and Shot?

Many gunners say they don't care if their dogs are not steady to wing and shot. But if you will ever want to get anywhere in field trials, steadiness is a necessity, and it has advantages in hunting too. The steady dog does not spoil shots by driving off other birds in his mad dash or risk being peppered with shot in his close pursuit of low rising birds. Moreover he is much more reliably staunch than the dog that has not been trained to be steady. The dog that is "only staunch" is much more liable to break when things go awry—when the bird bobbles in the brush trying to get up, or runs in sight of the dog before flying, or when another dog charges by his point. There are no disadvantages. The steady dog marks a bird as well as a dog plunging through the cover. He may, in fact, have a better view, and he retrieves equally well when sent on to fetch. The real reason why more dogs are not made steady to wing and shot may well be that this is a part of dog training that separates the men from the boys.

However that may be, you have decided that you want to make your dog a truly polished performer. If, after thorough yard training, you used the methods outlined for developing staunchness, you have laid a good foundation. Once in a long while a dog comes along who will become reliably steady with only the discipline required to teach and enforce the command "Whoa". You may think that yours is one of these because he will now stand steady while you go ahead of him and flush the bird. But it is one thing to be steady under these circumstances and another thing to be steady when the handler is not standing guard.

Keep in mind that in developing staunchness you worked with the help of one of your dog's strongest instincts—the instinct to pause and pinpoint the quarry before springing, which all pointing dogs have in varying degrees. In making your dog steady you are working *against* his equally strong instinct to chase and catch fleeing game. Stronger discipline is frequently required to make him understand that, although on fire with his inherent urge to chase, he must not do so, no matter what the circumstances or where you are at the moment.

Generations of dog trainers have made dogs steady with check-cords and choke or spiked collars, yanking them off their feet when they broke, or giving a few lashes on the belly for failure to obey "Whoa". A slingshot loaded with a pebble or BB shot and even thrown sticks have been used to advantage by trainers with good aim.

But if you can get an electronic trainer, why bother with these old methods, even though they have produced good results for years? You can be sure of one thing; they will take a lot more time and work.

With the electronic trainer you can use a method that will teach your dog not only to stand rock steady for a bird you flush in front of his point, but to stop in his tracks for a bird flying near him for any other reason.

Get about a dozen pigeons. Put a few in your hunting coat and take your dog and electronic trainer afield. Bobwhite quail could be used, but pigeons are better because they will not land nearby. If you must use quail, use strong flyers and be ready to grab the check-cord.

Put the electronic collar on the dog and let him run and hunt to take the edge off his initial enthusiasm. Then, as the dog makes a cast by you, release a pigeon. As your dog chases lustily, say nothing, but shock him. The dog may jump, but continue chasing a ways. Never mind, say nothing, and go back to hunting until the dog comes by you again. Then throw out another pigeon. The dog will chase again, perhaps more slowly. Once more, keep your mouth shut but shock the dog as he pursues the bird. Toss out another pigeon as the dog comes by you the third time. On the third bird there is a chance that the dog will stop and let the bird fly off. If he doesn't, shock again, and repeat with a fourth bird. I doubt if he will chase it, but if he does, get more pigeons and keep on tossing and shocking until he will no longer chase.

However many pigeons it takes, don't try to help your dog by ordering "Whoa". Let him chase until he abandons the practice of his own accord. Shock him every time he chases, but continue to say nothing. The psychology of this method is that the dog associates the shock with a bird in flight, not with you or a bird on the ground. And once he voluntarily stops chasing, you have him conquered. Put him in the car and go home.

The next time out, toss more birds, but do not shock him unless necessary. If he starts to chase, order "Whoa", and shock him only if he fails to obey. If your dog is slow to get the message, keep repeating. But my bet is that, if your dog has been properly yard-trained to whoa, you will not have to shock him at all in this second session.

The same procedure can be used on wild birds, but it will take more time if they are not plentiful. Even if it does take more time, wild birds are better than quail for this lesson. Unless you are very quick in administering the shock and grabbing the check-cord to prevent it, your dog will catch a short flying quail before you can stop him.

When working on wild birds, let the dog hunt until game is found. Whether the dog points or simply runs up the bird, shock him, saying nothing, as he chases the flying bird. Three or four finds will usually do the trick.

If you use pigeons, when the time comes that your dog will not chase them, leave him in the kennel for a few days. In the meantime, get some strong flying pheasants or quail. In your next session, toss these, just as you did the pigeons. The chances are that your dog will chase the first one you throw up, perhaps two. If he does, say nothing but shock him lightly. On the third bird you throw, if he starts to move shout "Whoa". He will stop.

Now you are ready to try your dog on birds on the ground. Put the dog in the car for a few minutes; I recommend 15. Meanwhile, put out a few quail for him to point. Put the electronic collar on the dog, but plan not to use it unless you have to. Work your dog upwind to a bird to secure a point or a flush, hopefully a point. When your dog scents game and pauses, say "Whoa" and he will point or stop. Here again I recommend that you have a helper to flush the bird. As it flies away, command "Whoa" if the dog makes a move to surge. This will probably stop him, but if it doesn't *and the bird is in the air* shock him lightly to stop him. If the bird runs before flying and the dog chases, stop him with the check-cord if necessary to prevent a catch, but withhold any shock until the bird is in the air. Remember that you should avoid shocking a dog approaching a bird on the ground. Work him on about three more birds, steadying the dog with a "Whoa" if you need to, but not shocking him unless absolutely necessary. Then load him in the car and go home.

Once the chase is out of your dog, use "Whoa" to mold perfection. Put the trainer away and do not use it again for this purpose if you can avoid it. In the lesson on staunchness you taught your dog not to flush and now he is trained to stand at wing and shot until heeled away or sent on. But you want him to do these things with confidence and style, not with signs of intimidation and uncertainty. This is where the difference between "the men and the boys" shows up; merely taking the chase out is easy with the electronic trainer. But in the molding of perfection, the personalities of both dog and handler are involved. Each dog is an individual case. You can be sure that as you continue to work on birds your dog will make mistakes at times. Patience is a necessity. Losing your temper or overly harsh discipline will work against the confidence you are seeking to build.

Use the electronic trainer only as a last resort when all else fails. For a moderately intelligent dog which has disobediently

flushed or chased, take a firm grip on his collar when you catch
him. Lift him off his feet and shake him hard four times. As you
set him down on the fourth shake, say "Whoa" harshly. Let the
dog stand quietly for a minute and repeat. A few such episodes
will accomplish the purpose. It is a much more certain cure than
whipping, and it will not make your dog timid on birds if you say
"Whoa" only once with each shaking. Angry and repeated shouting is much more liable to make your dog fearful of birds than is
the discomfort of his punishment.

How Should I Train My Dog to Back?

Show me a man who isn't thrilled when he sees dogs backing on
sight—stopping without command to honor the point of another
dog—and I will show you a man who doesn't really care about
pointing dogs. Some dogs do this instinctively and do it with style
and intensity. You cannot teach your dog to back instinctively if
it isn't in him to do so. But you can train him, through use of
"Whoa" and appropriate discipline, to understand that this is
another situation in which he must stop in his tracks and stand
until ordered on. Whoa your dog whenever he should back and
in time he may acquire the habit and do it without command.

Lest this sound too simple, let me warn you that unless your
dog is a natural backer the sight of another dog on point may have
just the opposite effect on him. Some dogs are overcome with
desire to charge by and steal the point, if not grab the bird. Or
your dog may circle the dog on point to hunt elsewhere. Although
your dog knows what "Whoa" means, discipline may be required.

If you have a friend with a good staunch dog, get him to work
with you. Put a bird out, and when your friend's dog is pointing
bring on your dog dragging a long check-cord. It is assumed that
by now you have enough control of your dog to keep him working
close to you. Approach the pointing dog head on into the wind
so that by the time your dog comes into normal backing range he
will also be getting bird scent (the more wind the better for
teaching backing). When you are sure that your dog has seen the
point, and he has not stopped, order "Whoa" sternly and grab
the check-cord. Jerk hard enough to take the dog off his feet.
Require your dog to be steady as the other handler flushes the
bird; then heel your dog away and put him back in the car for a

The handler of the pointing Vizsla on left readies his blank pistol as the German Shorthaired Pointer in back honors the point.

while. In early lessons do this each time between backs. It somehow changes the dog's outlook so that when you bring him out again he is more amenable to training, rather than just wanting to run and hunt.

The backing lesson is another place where the electronic trainer is easier than the older methods. You simply substitute a light shock for upsetting the dog's apple cart with the check-cord when he fails to obey your command to whoa. Put the electronic collar around the dog's belly for this, not on his neck.

If your dog will whoa on command when he sees another dog pointing—or when he reaches the stage where he will do so—do not flip him with the check-cord or shock him. You cannot force him to back without command if you want him to look good doing it. Mold him with the whoa command until he acquires the habit and will do it automatically.

But keep your voice handling at a minimum. One "Whoa" should be enough to stop your dog. Don't forget that the front dog hears you too, and a lot of shouting is confusing and upsetting to him. Front dogs can, and not infrequently do, go bad from this.

Give backing training in very small doses. Dogs back mainly from surprise, and surprise has a habit of growing stale.

Do I hear someone saying, "How can I teach backing when I have only my own dog to work with?" Don't despair. There is a very effective way you can do it with your dog alone.

"Judas Priest" is your answer. Who, or what, is Judas Priest?

It is a lifesize silhouette of a dog on point, jig-sawed out of a sheet of plywood. If you need a pattern, lay your dog down on wrapping paper and draw his outline with his tail lifted in pointing position. Paint the wooden dog mostly white with black, brown, or yellow markings for contrast. Mount it standing on a piece of plank, and it is ready for action.

Don't worry if the wooden dog you make is not a work of art. Your dog is not an art critic. I got the idea for Judas one time when I was working a dog on a very windy day. The wind had blown a newspaper against a wire fence and when the dog saw it, he froze on point.

For use with your Judas, you need a way of putting out a bird so that you can release it and make it fly away by remote control. There are a variety of ways to do this. If money is no object, you can buy an electronically controlled game bird releaser. Or you can use an ordinary spring-release cage and attach strong twine to the release lever. As I will discuss later, I have now modified my Judas to include a built-in bird box with a long string tied to the release door.

But if you want to keep things at the simplest, least expensive level, you can, in just a few minutes, build the effective remote-control bird releaser I call "Flush-Away". Take a piece of plywood about 14 inches long by 8 inches wide. Cut one of the 8-in. sides to a flat V so that the plywood is a little longer in the center than at the edges. Make the plywood into a little sled by nailing on the under side strips of wood about an inch high for runners. Bore a hole in the point of the V so that you can attach 30 feet of ¼-in. rope for pulling the sled. Cut an oval opening in the center of the plywood. If you will be using pigeons, make the opening 6 inches the long way of the plywood by 5 inches wide. If you will be using quail, both the plywood and the opening could of course be smaller, but I would make Flush-Away big enough for pigeons and try to get some. In any case, shape a piece of ½-in. hardware cloth into a dome like a derby hat or tea strainer and mount it over the oval opening. Make the dome about the height of a teacup so that the bird can stick its head up into it, increasing the scent. When you pull the rope Flush-Away slides over the bird. This not only frees the bird but disturbs it enough so that it will want to fly away.

Now you are ready for the backing lesson. Put Judas out in a

Two young dogs get a simultaneous lesson in backing with the help of "Judas Priest" and "Flush Away." Paul and Fletcher Mull handling.

The "Judas" dog, with built-in bird releaser, is a tool for many uses as well as training in backing.

light clearing in the cover, where your dog won't see it from a distance but will come on it unexpectedly. Put your pigeon or quail under Flush-Away a foot or two ahead of Judas in the direction from which the wind is blowing. String Flush-Away's pull rope downwind past Judas in the direction from which you will be bringing your dog.

Go and get your dog and work him, dragging the check-cord, into the wind toward Judas. As mentioned earlier, the more wind the better for backing lessons. If your dog backs on sight of Judas, so much the better. If not, work him closer until he gets bird scent and points. Stroke your dog. Lean down quietly and flush the bird by pulling the rope to Flush-Away. Keeping your dog in place, step forward and lay Judas on its side. Then take your dog back to the car.

While your dog is pondering his experience, reload Flush-Away and set Judas upright. Then repeat the performance. Your dog may seem not even to see Judas the first few times, but he is nevertheless learning that the wooden dog means "bird ahead." After a few repetitions you will see him react when Judas comes in view. It may be only a momentary pause or he may almost pussyfoot. Then command "Whoa" and proceed as before, stroking the dog, flushing the bird, and turning Judas to the ground. As your dog progresses in training, you will be able to walk ahead of him to flush the bird with your foot before turning Judas over.

Don't overdo it in the first session, and in later sessions look for new hiding places for Judas if you can find them.

As they say in the TV commercial, "Try it; you'll like it". When your dog will honor Judas Priest he will honor a live dog just as quickly. And when the opportunity comes to back a live dog, you will be past the danger of harming the front dog by undue voice handling. There will be no need for it.

With a little of what car dealers would call optional equipment, your Judas can be used in many ways in your training program. It can be useful in following my instructions on introducing your dog to the gun. It can supplement your yard training on "whoa" and help in teaching your dog to retrieve. I now use my wooden dog for all of these things and all the while the dogs are having fun and learning to back.

Judas was modified by cutting an indentation in the wooden

dog's back, five inches long by five inches deep. In this indentation was set a square bird-box, plywood top and bottom and on the front and rear ends. The sides are flap doors, wire on light frames, hinged at the bottom with easy opening catches at the top. A string is attached to each catch and tied to a single string running 30 to 40 feet to the rear of the wooden dog.

When a young dog—six months or older—has been taken afield enough times to have had the fun of finding and chasing a few loose birds—two or three times or enough to get him hunting— he is ready to be introduced to Judas.

With the wooden dog standing majestically in light cover, a pigeon in the bird box and a helper to pull the strings, bring on the young dog on a long check-cord. Work the dog upwind to Judas Priest, with the breeze blowing from Judas into the dog's face. Start from a place where Judas is not visible, and let the dog range the length of the check-cord. When you come to a place where your dog notices Judas, he may freeze on point. If so, so much the better, but if he doesn't, keep working toward Judas until the dog catches bird scent. Then signal your helper to pull the string, opening both doors of the bird box and letting the pigeon fly out either side. Let your pup chase to the end of your check-cord, without admonition or correction except for being stopped by the cord. Then take him back to the starting point and repeat the performance.

Do this eight or ten times, with your helper resetting the cage with a new pigeon each time. Whether or not your dog froze on his first encounter with Judas, he is probably now at least halting momentarily when he catches sight of the wooden dog.

Now you are ready to introduce the gun. Have your helper use a .22 pistol with a foreign, crimped blank. American blanks are too loud at this stage. When you signal your helper to release the bird, have him fire the blank as the pigeon flies away. If your dog is not stopping voluntarily at the sight of Judas, hold him with the check-cord and a "whoa" until the bird is released, and then let him chase merrily as before, with your helper holding fire until the dog is in pursuit. Repeat this two or three times.

By now your dog is honoring Judas to some degree, is eager to see the bird fly, and ignores the crack of the pistol as he happily pursues the flight. He is now ready for bigger things.

For the next step you need a shotgun and a helper who is a good shot, for you are going to ask him to knock down the bird in flight. Have him use a .20 gauge shotgun if available. But whatever the gauge, make sure that only light-load shells are shot.

At this point I switch from a pigeon to a Bobwhite quail. But when quail are not available, you can continue to use pigeons. You bring on the young dog as before. When the dog honors voluntarily or on caution, signal your helper to release the bird. If you are using quail, the quail may walk out of the box and drop to the ground. If so, have your helper flush the bird and drop it in flight. Let go of the rope and let the dog run out to retrieve. If your dog has trouble locating the fallen bird, guide him to the spot with the check-cord. If the dog doesn't want to give up the retrieved bird, blow in his ear.

Repeat this exercise, but only on one more bird that day. Do not shoot more than two birds a day for the first three workouts. After two birds, the dog will be too excited for further training. Kennel him until another day.

By the time you have shot six birds over the dog over a three or four day period, no amount of gunfire will disturb him. At the beginning, the light blank when fired is 30 or more feet away from the dog, who is so engrossed in Judas Priest and the flight of the bird that he ignores the crack of the pistol. And by the time you introduce the shotgun with a light load, he will ignore that too. Even dogs that seem a little soft to gunfire at the beginning soon forget their timidity in the joy of the chase and retrieve.

After the dog has had a half a dozen birds shot over him with the fun of retrieving, you can substitute a live dog for Judas Priest. The chances are that the young dog will honor voluntarily, but if he doesn't, use the check-cord and a firm but quiet "whoa". In either case, there is no danger of upsetting the pointing dog, which can happen all too often when there is a lot of commotion and shouting at a dog being trained close by.

This program is not a substitute for yard training, and at its completion your dog will not yet be ready for field trials requiring steadiness to wing and shot. But you have given your pup the big picture and conditioned him to every aspect of what will be expected of him later on. Combining it with yard training, you can build a solid foundation for the dog's future development as a field trial competitor or satisfying gun dog. Experienced trainers know that you are only inviting frustration for yourself and the dog if you attempt the ultimate training in steadiness to wing and shot before the dog has been schooled to "whoa" and the other basic commands by thorough yard training.

But yard training is no great fun for either man or dog. Dogs enjoy their workouts with the wooden dog, and by laying a foundation in backing and retrieving, as well as conditioning the dog to the gun, these workouts give you a head start on developing a completely satisfactory dog.

If you are anxious to get started with a young pup, you can get benefits from Judas Priest any time after the dog is six months old and has learned to look for birds. But other than limiting his range with a check-cord, avoid any attempts at discipline until the dog has matured enough for yard training.

How Can I Train My Dog to Retrieve?

If you mean force training to retrieve, I am not the man to answer. This type of training has never interested me, and I have done none of it. However, I can tell you ways to encourage and develop the retrieving instinct, which exists to some extent in most dogs of all pointing breeds. In fact it is so strong in many that they retrieve with little or no training. Perhaps they cannot be relied on as certainly to retrieve under all circumstances as a force-trained dog. They might not be as apt to win in a field trial requiring retrieving. But what they do they do happily and they please the men who shoot birds over them.

But all pointing dogs are not blessed with the instinct to this degree. If yours is one that isn't, try this. When you shoot down a bird and your dog goes for it, turn quickly as he get to it and walk away. Frequently, surprised by this action, the dog will pick up the bird and start to follow. Praise the dog if he picks up the bird and starts with it, even though he comes only part way. Don't try to get more results out of that bird. Go on hunting and try it again when you shoot another bird. Keep trying, even if you have a few failures.

If you enjoy working with your dog and don't mind experimenting with tactics to entice him to retrieve, get a live game bird. A pigeon could be used, but a quail or other live game bird is better. Hobble the bird's legs and attach a 20-ft. kite string. Throw the bird out into the grass and order "Fetch". As the dog finds the bird, draw it slowly toward you. The moving bird will excite the dog, and he will probably pick it up. Continue to pull in the cord slowly. If the dog holds the bird, good. But if he drops it after a few feet, keep on drawing it slowly toward you, and the dog will follow. Praise the dog when he gets to you and try it again. But don't repeat more than half a dozen times in one session, and go to a different area of your field each time you throw the bird. Fresh scent and new areas make it more interesting for the dog.

If the live gamebird on a string seems to get you nowhere, try this procedure. Cut a 10-inch piece from a broomstick or other round wood, and with a power saw cut three grooves the length of this piece, ¼-in. deep by ¼-in. wide. Pack these grooves with a mixture of bacon grease and cooked liver. Then, at a time when your dog doesn't have a full stomach, throw the stick out on a 20-foot string and order him to fetch. The scent and taste of the broomstick guarantee that he will pick it up. Repeat "Fetch" and slowly draw the stick in to you as the dog holds on. When the dog reaches your feet, blow in his ear and he will drop the stick. Give him a morsel of cooked liver and praise him. Repeat half a dozen times each day, always rewarding the dog with a bit of liver and praise. Then try a live bird on a string again and gauge your progress.

As a substitute for the slotted broomstick, you can use a hollow length of bamboo of comparable size. Cut three slots with a saber-saw and pack the hollow with the appetizer until it oozes through the slots. In place of the liver and bacon-fat mixture you can use a canned dog food that you know your dog will gulp with gusto. I prefer the liver and bacon mixture because all dogs seem to love it.

When using a bird on the string, always use a clean, healthy bird. Many dogs dislike a saliva coated bird, especially if another dog has mouthed it. There are also dogs that just do not like a dead bird, and will not pick one up even though quick to grab one with a quiver of life still in it. Thankfully these are rare, because I do not know how they can be made to retrieve dead birds short of force training.

5

Problems

Gunshyness

This is a major fault created by owners, and is more easily avoided than corrected. It is important to introduce the gun to the dog properly (See Chapter 3), but even dogs conditioned can be made gunshy through thoughtlessness.

A sensitive young dog is taken out on opening day, and the owner has brought along a couple of hunting companions. All three hunters are armed with three-shot automatics with magnum loads. A bird flushes ahead of the young dog. It's a long shot, but all empty their guns. The noise is terrific and no bird is down. The dog has never before heard a barrage like it—probably has not even previously heard the boom of a single magnum—but he seems unaffected. The hunters move on toward the marked bird and flush another one, with which the dog is not involved. Again shots ring out. The owner calls in the dog to find the dead bird. While the dog is searching, there is another flush elsewhere, and again there is a barrage of high-powered shells. By now the dog is unstrung and goes to his master, or perhaps runs back to the car. If he does the latter, it is probably the end of a good hunting dog.

*Never fire a shotgun directly over a young, untrained dog. This creates
gunshyness.*

Moral: When shooting over a young dog on his first hunt, shoot
only birds that the dog has pointed, or at least has been involved
with. Until several birds have been knocked down to give the
dog a picture of what it's all about, limit the firing to one or two
shots at a time, and shoot only light loads.

When game is scarce, a dog tires and loses interest toward the
end of a long day. In this state he becomes especially susceptible
to gunshyness. Avoid overtiring a dog on his introduction to hunting. Let the dog find out what hunting is about in small doses.
Avoid artillery barrages until the dog has had a part in five or six
kills, which will usually suffice to make him ignore any amount
of gunfire.

Gunshyness alone can be overcome. The real difficulty is that
the gunshy dog frequently becomes birdshy also. The owner,
hoping that the gunshyness will go away if enough birds are shot
over the dog, continues to hunt him. The dog learns that the flush
of a bird is immediately followed by the noise he dreads. Now
he has two fears, and wilts and turns away from bird scent. If a
dog reaches this point, the best thing to do is to look for a new
dog. It is very unlikely that the dog will ever overcome his fear.

But if you will stop trying to hunt your gunshy dog before you have made him fear birds as well as guns, there is a way of overcoming his problem. With a dog that still enjoys finding birds, your chance of success is almost total.

You will need a helper, a blank pistol that shoots .22 crimped blanks of the acorn variety, a .22 rifle loaded with the shot commonly called rat shot, a .20-gauge shotgun with light-load shells, and a check-cord.

Tell your helper to keep 300 feet away from the dog unless called closer or waved off, and to shoot only when you signal.

Bring your dog into the field on the check-cord to hunt or just mess around. When you are about 300 feet away from your helper, signal him to fire a .22 crimped blank. Watch your dog. If he shows signs of fear, pay no attention. The check-cord will keep the dog from bolting. Keep walking, showing no concern, until the dog regains his composure and resumes hunting or messing around. Keeping your distance from your assistant, signal him to fire another crimped blank, and as before, keep your dog from bolting with the check-cord but otherwise show no concern. After the dog's attention has returned to his surroundings, signal for a third blank. You are done with the helper for this outing. Pretend to hunt for a while, and then put the dog away.

Next time out, the next day if possible, repeat the procedure and continue on succeeding outings until the dog only looks up with curiosity at the sound of the blank pistol. Then have your helper fire the blank when only about 150 feet from the dog, and repeat daily until the dog pays no attention to the shot, accepting the noise of the .22 blank as a part of being in the field.

Now have your helper carry, along with the blank pistol, the .22 rifle loaded with rat shot. Rat shot, although sounding a little like a baby shotgun, makes a noise dogs seem rather to like. First have your helper fire the pistol to which the dog has grown accustomed. Then, a little later, have him fire the rat shot. If the dog reacts unfavorably, keep on walking. Moments later shoot the rifle again. If the dog takes the rat shot reasonably well, have a third shot fired and then quit for the day.

On succeeding workouts, have the pistol fired several times first followed by several well-spaced shots from the rifle. Don't proceed faster than the dog will accept, and continue interchanging until the sounds of the blank and the rat shot at 300 feet or less mean nothing to the dog.

When all is going well, add the .20 gauge shotgun with light loads to your helper's armament. Have him shoot it not more than twice, well away from the dog, with four or five minutes between shots. Keep walking between shots, and repeat for several days until your dog comes to accept these distant shot-gun reports too.

For the next step, put out five or six quail in a wire cage in light cover. Arm your helper with all three weapons and station him about a hundred feet from the birds, ready to move in quickly on signal. Course your dog on a check-cord up to the birds. This is a time when you are not trying to get your dog to point. If he does when he scents the birds, jostle the cage to make the birds flutter and excite the dog so that he will jump in and attempt to grab the cage or run around it. As he does, signal your helper to move in, firing the blank pistol and then the rat shot as he moves. If the dog stops moving, joggle the cage with your foot or hand to re-excite him. While he is jumping at the cage, release the latch and let several birds escape. As the dog chases, have your helper fire the shotgun not more than twice, hopefully knocking down a bird. Let the dog retrieve or mouth it. Make a great deal of him, and quit for the day.

Repeat the next time out, and this time the dog will probably be eager to jump in without encouragement. Condition the dog as before, with your helper firing lighter loads as he approaches and knocking down a bird with the shotgun at the flush.

By now your dog is almost conditioned to accept gunfire as a way of life, but there is a final step. Next time, set two strong flying quail about ten feet apart in light cover. Put them one behind the other, in line with your approach as you bring your dog into the wind. As you approach have your helper fire rat shot a couple of times and be ready to move in with the shotgun when called on. When the dog scents the first bird, hold him on the check-cord if he doesn't point. Direct your assistant to move in to flush, not the first bird, but the second one, ten feet ahead, coming in from the side so as not to block the dog's view.

You want your helper to flush and knock down the second bird so that the shotgun blast will not be directly over your dog's head. Let the dog rush in to mouth or retrieve the bird, and praise him. Repeat the procedure and call it a day.

In this session and for several more workouts, shoot only once at each bird. If the dog shows some uneasiness, he will recoup quickly if only one shot is fired. And don't kill more than two birds. The excitement of the gun and mouthing or retrieving the birds can be mentally exhausting for some dogs. Quit while your dog is still eager to find game.

After several of these workouts, you can shoot a bird directly over the dog, pointing or held on a check-cord. One shot only.

Now you are ready to take your dog hunting. But until you have killed six birds over your dog limit gunfire to two shots per bird—better yet only one until you are sure gunfire has no effect. And another caution: don't shoot at birds not found by the dog. If the dog is not involved with the flush, pass up the shot. Shots for which the dog sees no reason can be unsettling.

Bide your time until you have knocked down half a dozen birds that the dog has found for you. He will then accept gunfire anywhere, and jump happily when he sees you with your gun because it means you are going hunting. Once your dog's hangup on guns is cured, don't worry about its returning. A dog is gunshy or he isn't. There is no in between.

In all this, you have been overcoming gunshyness, not training for staunchness or steadiness to flush. Now that you have succeeded, training for staunchness can begin.

If for lack of time or facilities you can't cure your gunshy dog yourself, turn him over to a trainer who specializes in this problem. Don't let anybody talk you into the starvation or thirst diets that some recommend for gunshyness. They are pure sadism.

Running Too Wide

Every dog has a natural speed and range, just as you have a natural gait which is not like your neighbor's and may even differ from your brother's. Dogs run wide for two reasons. The first is because that is their natural range; it has been bred into them. The other is disobedience.

The electronic trainer can be very helpful to you in spelling out the range of the erratic disobedient dog. You can also use it to deter wide running in the dog that does it because it is his natural range, but he won't hunt happily.

It doesn't take great skill to decide which category your dog falls into. The wide-running obedient dog runs to objectives that may be far distant, but he will not lose contact with you. He will look for your directions and comply with them. If your dog is of this type and you want a closer working dog, you and he will both be happier if you change ownership and find a dog more suited to your requirements.

Catwalking on Point

Catwalking, or stalking in on game after establishing point, is costly to the hunter in the loss of good shots and to the field trialer in loss of placements. It is easily corrected. Arm yourself with a slingshot and a few pebbles, marbles or BB shot. When, after establishing point, the dog lifts one foot slowly over the other, be prepared. Hit him in the flank with your pellet and say "Whoa" once. Be ready for a second shot.

This method rarely fails, but if it does, use an electronic trainer. Strap the collar around the dog's flank, ahead of his hindquarters, with the contact points touching his belly lightly. It will not impede his movement and he can run and hunt freely. When the dog points and begins to catwalk, touch the button *lightly*. The dog will jump and as he jumps say "Whoa" harshly just once.

Do I hear someone objecting, "But you have said never to shock a dog approaching a bird on the ground?" This is one of the rare exceptions to the rule. It can be done with the collar points touching the dog's belly. The dog will not associate the shock of the collar with the bird ahead but with the jab of some briar or stick in the cover. You will find other examples in this book when I recommend attaching the electronic collar to the dog's belly rather than the neck. In these instances do not think you could achieve the same results with the collar on the neck. This could lead to disaster. In no case have I ever had bad results when using the collar on the belly as directed.

A couple of plinks with the slingshot or four or five tickles with the electronic trainer are usually enough to provide a cure. The dog learns that those extra steps bring unpleasantness.

Wildness After Frequent Finds

Frequent finds excite a dog. He picks up speed and overruns birds because he is running too fast for his nose or out of sheer exuberance. Your job is to slow him down. The electronic trainer is the best training aid for this. When the dog picks up speed, shock him and say "Slow". Do it whenever he starts going too fast, always repeating the command. He will soon get the message and work slowly. Carry the trainer on workouts until the dog will obey the command without the shock. Depending on the dog, you may achieve your goal in a few workouts, or you may have to carry the trainer for several weeks, but it is not a hard problem to correct.

But keep alert. You want to avoid shocking the dog as he is about to point or flush a bird. This is another time when I recommend having the collar around the dog's belly rather than around his neck. It works well and minimizes the danger of an inadvertent shock just as a bird flushes.

Trailing Birds Too Fast

Birds that run through the cover after being pointed—pheasants are notorious for this—have unstrung many a good pointing dog with results frustrating to the owner. The dog, when sent on, trails too fast, precipitating a flush out of gun range.

In by-gone days it took experience on many, many such birds and great perseverance on the part of the trainer working with the tools then available to him—the voice, a dragging chain, a rope, or a whip—to teach the dog to proceed at a reasonable speed.

If you have used the electronic trainer to teach your dog to understand and obey the command "Slow" (see "Wildness After Frequent Finds"), the command will help you with this problem also. When a bird runs from your dog's point and you send the dog on, caution "Slow". If he tends to pick up speed later, repeat the command. At intervals command "Whoa" to enable you to get into firing position before sending the dog ahead again. Do this especially whenever the dog gives any sign that he is approaching game.

If your dog has not already learned the "Slow" command, it can be taught now with the electronic trainer, but very close attention and good judgment are required on your part.

When a bird has run off, send the dog on. He will move slowly at first, then pick up speed. When he speeds up, say "Slow".

Never having had this command before, the dog will ignore it. Say "Slow" once more and shock the dog *lightly*. It will bring him to a stop or nearly so. Encourage him to go on and repeat the command "Slow". As he picks up speed, say "Slow, slow" and tickle him lightly again with the electronic trainer. Keep the dog moving forward, but slow him down as needed with the command "Slow" and the lightest possible shock. After a few tingles he will be moving cautiously.

However, you must be very observant. Study the cover to anticipate where the bird might flush, and study your dog for any sign that he is nearing the game. If in doubt, whoa the dog until you get into position. Whenever you send the dog on, there is a calculated risk that the bird may flush. Anticipate this and do not shock the dog as the bird leaves the ground; this could make him a blinker.

Teaching the dog to obey the "Slow" command is the key to the problem. When the bird takes to its legs, move the dog forward at a speed you can comfortably follow. Whoa the dog to a point at intervals to let you get into shooting position; then move the dog on again. With experience the dog will come to gauge the distance to the bird, moving when it moves, pointing when it stops. But do not expect to accomplish this in one easy lesson. It will take repeated workouts on running birds before you can leave the electronic trainer home. And as long as you may have to use it for this purpose, it is important that you shock the dog as lightly as possible—you want to slow him down, not bring him running back to you—and take great care that you do not shock the dog coincident with a flush. Here, again, I recommend having the collar on the dog's belly rather than on his neck.

With patience, there is another way to achieve the same end without using a shock collar. Recently I worked two Boykin Spaniels that would point and handle birds if the birds would lay tight. But if the birds ran, it was a whole new ball game. Their little rear ends would wiggle, and their spaniel breeding would take over as they rushed in to flush. Dealing with dogs in which pointing is not a primary instinct, I did not wish to use the shock collar lest I kill their acquired talent.

I got a strong cock pheasant and tied his legs a little apart with a short string, to the middle of which I fastened another string about 30 feet long. The string between the bird's legs was long enough to let it run, and if it flew I could ground it with the long string. In this fashion, the bird was allowed to travel for about 300 feet through medium high cover. Then I picked up the pheasant and set out a pigeon.

Then I brought on a Boykin Spaniel on a check-cord, guiding him upwind to where he would pick up the start of the pheasant's trail. As the scent excited him, I cautioned "slow, slow" over and over, using the check-cord when necessary and frequently whoaing him to a stop before letting him proceed. When he pointed the pigeon, I flushed it and shot. For two weeks, I repeated this daily, and it produced results.

This is a procedure effective with any dog that points, and it can be expanded in an exercise your dog will enjoy. After running the pheasant through 300 feet of cover, picking it up and planting a pigeon, carry the pheasant another 100 feet or more and put it down again. Run it 150 feet or so this time, and set another pigeon. Work your dog to where he will point the first pigeon, flush it and shoot, and take your dog on to pick up the next trail. Excited by the first find, your dog will be eager to rush ahead, but you will restrain him as before with the check-cord and the command "slow". You can have more points by setting out more pigeons at intervals along the pheasant's route. At first you will probably have to whoa your dog into a point, and so that you will know where he should pick up the scent of the planted birds it is wise to leave some sort of a marker, a piece of paper, broken twig, or twisted grass.

As the dog advances in training you can let the check-cord trail and then remove it altogether. For the first few times without restraint, however, don't plant any birds; run your dog on the pheasant trail only, to avoid his catching birds. When you are satisfied that your dog has learned to trail at a reasonable pace and point where he should, put out a Bobwhite quail where the pheasant trail stops as a final test.

Trailing Another Dog

Except in young puppies that have not yet learned to hunt, this fault is usually man made. Avoid it by not running a young dog with a faster, more experienced dog. Run young dogs of about the same age, experience, and range, together. They may trail and play for a few minutes at break-away, but will soon find more interesting things to take their attention. Avoid bare fields that encourage foot racing. Avoid running kennel mates together. Run a young dog with a dog that is not a regular playmate.

If your young dog has already formed the habit of trailing, run him with two other dogs of similar range and experience. He won't know which to chase.

Getting the dog on game, to love hunting on his own, is the best cure. Once he loves finding birds, teach him the "look for birds" signal (see Chapter 2). Then, if he trails momentarily, give him this signal. He will break off to hunt, and then you can send him on.

If time and such means do not correct the fault, use an electronic trainer. Let the dog trail for a good ten minutes. Then tickle him ever so lightly and command "No". If, as is probable, he resumes trailing in a few minutes, repeat. Several such workouts and you will be able to break the dog away merely by commanding "No". But use the electronic trainer lightly and sparingly.

Running the Track at Field Trials

You can build this fault into a dog without ever entering a field trial if you are thoughtless in your training activities. You have an area where you work your dog, regularly following the same trail to a spot where, because the cover is better or it is more convenient, you plant birds for the dog to point. Each time out you run the dog around the trail for exercise and then swing him into your private birdfield. The better a dog knows an area, the wider he will run. Your dog is soon running wider and has learned what he will find at the end of the trail. He sees no need to wait for you, way back and out of touch with him. By the time you get there he has found the game and acquired a new habit. If you must always use the same area, at least vary your route. Release birds in different places each time, and the dog, not knowing where he will find them, will search all the way.

In field trials the habit is created by owners of winning puppies or well-finished derbies who just can't resist trying for two wins in the same trial. Besides running in the puppy event, they will run their hot prospect as a derby too. Or they want to see if their well-trained derby can't also place as a shooting dog or all-age.

The dog runs over much the same course in each event, and finds that the things he loves most are at the end of it. The better the bird dog, the better he remembers where he found birds, and soon that is the place he heads for. With more and more clubs liberating birds around the course rather than merely in the bird-field, the danger of creating this fault is decreasing. But think twice before entering the same dog more than once in the same bird-field trial.

If your dog already has the habit, look for a fun trial or a trial where club officials will allow you to run your dog around the course as a non-competitor at the close of a recognized stake. Then buy or borrow an electronic trainer. Let your dog wear the dummy collar day and night for several days before the event.

At the trial, when you take the dog out of the box, rub and handle him and in the process quietly substitute the active collar for the dummy. Cast your dog off at the starting line as you would normally. Let him ramble, but watch him closely. The moment he shows a sign of heading for the birdfield, signal him to turn. If you were right in guessing that he was about to rush for the birdfield, he will refuse. Shock him, more than a light touch but not enough to discourage him from hunting. Proceed nonchalantly until the dog builds up enough confidence to try it again; then repeat the procedure.

Many dogs can be corrected this way, but it may take more than one "trial" to do it. However, even if it is necessary to pay entry fees for stakes that you cannot compete in, it will be worth the cost to cure your dog of his bad habit.

When the time comes that you feel that you can trust your dog in a trial as a bonafide competitor, you may feel embarrassed to run him with the dummy collar, or might not be permitted to do so. Get a piece of lead slightly narrower than your dog's regular collar and about the weight of the dummy. Tape or rivet it inside the regular collar. Not all dogs are fooled by this, but many are, and on these it has enough of a sobering effect to maintain the handler's control.

Running to the Gallery

A field trialer works his dog from horseback in training for coming competitions. At the end of each workout he rides back to his station wagon or truck with his dog running ahead. The dog learns that heading for the rig means pick-up time.

Later at a one-course trial his dog runs through the birdfield to the cars parked conspicuously in the gallery, anticipating pick-up. It is so easy to avoid this that it is amazing that it happens. When you finish your workout, get off your horse several hundred yards from your car and cord the dog the rest of the way. Or salt an area corresponding to the birdfield near the car with birds, so that the dog will learn to look for birds near the car prior to pick-up. Then, after the dog has worked the birds, cord him to your car.

Flagging on Point

There are two causes of flagging on point. One is hereditary, the other man-made. They are easy to distinguish. The dog that flags because of the genes of some ancestor, perhaps four or five generations back, will wave his whole tail from the base up. If your dog does this, there is little hope. You will have to tolerate it or trade off the dog.

The man-made flagger moves the end of his tail, not the base. The dog is registering uncertainty, either because he has been left on point too long and is tiring, or from excessive handling on point. Owners are frequently guilty of the latter. They call "Whoa" too many times, or talk to the dog too much with expressions like "Careful, boy", "Easy, boy", etc. Or they stroke the dog and talk to him to get his tail up and rigid. The dog is waiting for the climax, the flush of the bird. It is slow in coming, and he finds an escape hatch.

When your dog points, or is found on point, it is good practice to call "Whoa" or "Point" once to stabilize him and let him know that you are approaching. But keep your mouth shut as you walk in to flush. If the dog makes any movement, from the flicker of an eye or ear to leg or tail movement, command "Whoa" harshly again, just once, and proceed to flush. If your dog will not stay on point without numerous cautions, you are the one who has failed. Go back to yard training and teach him what "Whoa" means.

If flagging has become a habit, here is the way to correct it. As you approach the dog on point, speak "Whoa" once. Ignore the flagging, keep your mouth shut, and walk in to flush. Stop just before you flush, and hiss through your teeth. Watch your dog. When he stops flagging stop hissing. If he starts again, hiss again and flush the bird. On each point, flush the bird reasonably quickly, and avoid keeping the dog standing too long after flush.

Study your dog. You will notice that he will point, then begin to flag. When, after calling "Whoa" or "Point" once, you get within 15 feet of the dog, hiss and he will stop flagging. A dog on point knows what usually follows. The hiss introduces an unknown element, and he tenses. Except for one "Whoa" and the hissing, keep your mouth shut, and there is a good chance that with experience and confidence the dog will overcome the weakening trait.

Pointing Dead

Owners are sometimes unhappy because their dogs will point a dead bird, but will not pick it up and retrieve. They should consider themselves lucky. I say this because a dog that will point dead will not bump or crowd a live bird. The dog would rather point than hold a bird in his mouth or see one in the air.

Retrieving is a pretty sight and desirable. Elsewhere in this book you will find suggestions for encouraging your dog to retrieve. But if you have no success, remember that it is a rare sight to see a man point a bird. However, many men have a back strong enough to lean down and pick up a bird that a dog has located and pointed dead.

Dropping on Point

This is a most difficult fault to correct. Most attempts to do so end in failure. The fault is often hereditary. There was a time when dropping for the shot was considered desirable, and dogs were trained to drop at the command of "Charge" if they did not do it without command. Now considered a weakness, it can be brought out by a handler who brandishes a flushing whip to deter the dog from chasing when the bird is flushed. Or it can be caused by the sensitivity of a dog's ears; dropping is his reflex action to the boom of a heavy charge. Whatever the cause, the dog that drops on point is like a person with abnormal fear of heights. Little can be done about it.

It sometimes helps to walk in to flush at a 45-degree angle, rather than directly past the dog, but this is impossible if the dog is close to the game. Many ideas have been tried, such as using a harness with points that will prick the dog's belly when he goes down, or putting the electronic shocker on his belly. Once in a while one may be successful, but on the whole such attempts meet with dismal failure.

If you have the dog only for hunting, letting him break shot when birds are killed will get him out of the habit. But when you try to steady the dog to shot again, he will usually revert to dropping.

If you are planning to run in field trials, the best and cheapest correction is to replace the dog.

Biting Birds

A young dog retrieving a bird is in a state near frenzy from excitement and happiness. The master is so eager to get the bird from the dog's mouth that a tugging contest ensues. The dog clamps down harder, tastes the meat, and starts chewing. The seed of a habit is planted.

If the master had only leaned down, said "Give", and blown directly into the dog's ear, the puppy would have dropped the bird into his hand. Most hard-mouthed dogs are created by the eagerness and seeming greediness of their handlers. Use discretion and a little breath blown into the dog's ear, and this bad trait will rarely develop.

Running Off with the Bird

Some dogs will rush to a downed bird and pick it up, but then run off with it. The way to correct this is to run your dog with a 30-foot check-cord trailing. When you shoot a bird, lay down your gun and pick up the cord. Call the dog to you, pulling him in hand over hand if necessary. The dog, all excited, won't bite the bird. When you get a firm hold on the dog, take the bird from him. If he doesn't want to let go, lean down and blow in his ear;

he will drop the bird immediately. Praise the dog no end, and let him smell the bird, but under no circumstances let him bite it. Then throw the bird out and let the dog retrieve again, following the same procedure. Don't throw the bird out more than twice; three retrieves is enough for one lesson.

You can do this while not actually hunting by shooting a liberated bird. But with a liberated bird you may find that the dog will drop it before you get him all the way to you, although very few dogs will drop a wild bird while being brought in. The conclusion I have reached after seeing dogs drop liberated birds repeatedly, particularly quail, is that commercial game-bird feed contains cod-liver oil or some other ingredient that gives the bird a flavor unpleasant to a dog.

Another way to correct this fault without shooting wild birds is to use a "tasty stick" loaded with a food the dog relishes, as described in Chapter 4 in the instructions for encouraging your dog to retrieve. Throw the stick out a short distance and let the dog follow and pick it up. Then by calling and pulling the check-cord if you have to, bring him to you. Take the stick away from him, blowing in his ear if necessary, and reward the dog with a morsel of the same food and praise. Repeat until the dog shows that he can be trusted to bring the stick in voluntarily. He will enjoy this game, and his learning will transfer to the field after the excitement of the first live bird or two.

Destroying Birds

Some bird-biters carry their bad trait to the point of literally destroying the bird. There is a sure cure for this which some may consider cruelty. It is strong medicine for a very serious fault, but it is much less cruel than the methods many hunters use. I have known people to twist a dog's leg, hit him with their gun butts, even stomp on the dog or kick him in their anger.

The method I suggest requires very few applications. It will make a dog a tender retriever for life, and if more widely used would save countless dogs from much more cruel treatment.

Take the dog hunting with a trailing check-cord attached. When you shoot down a bird, have a lighted cigar, cigaret or even a cigaret lighter ready. As the dog picks up the bird call him or, if necessary, pull him to you. Catch the dog firmly under the chin with one hand, and apply the hot end of the cigar, cigaret or lighter right into his nostril. The dog will spit out the bird. A few moments later throw out the bird and send the dog to fetch. If he is hard-headed, he may chew the bird while retrieving it, or he may stand off chewing and you will have to pull him to you. Either way, hold his head with one hand and apply the heat to the nostril again with the other. He will spit out the bird with a vengeance. Throw the bird out again. The dog will probably refuse to pick it up. Don't be concerned. Go hunting for another bird. On the next bird you shoot, repeat the procedure if it is necessary, but it rarely is. Usually the dog will run out and retrieve the bird without wetting a feather. If, although no longer chewing, he is still reluctant to give up the bird, blow into his ear.

A hard-headed dog requires more pressure of the hot brand; a sensitive dog needs less. But never has it been necessary to enact the lesson more than three times. It will not make the dog refuse to retrieve. The dog associates the pain with his chewing, and it is a lesson he never forgets.

The lesson can be taught during the off season by using a hobbled quail. Throw the quail the length of the check-cord and send the dog to fetch. But don't use a bird that has been mouthed or mutilated; use a live, healthy bird. Dogs dislike a bird covered with the saliva of another dog, and a mutilated bird is temptation to further chewing.

If your dog is one that stands off at a distance chewing, this method is hard to apply, especially without a check-cord. In this case, all you can do is walk to the dog and try to catch him.

Jumping In

I am talking now about a dog that has been yard trained to whoa, and is staunch until you approach. But just before you get into position to shoot, he jumps in and flushes the bird.

When the dog flushes, go to him and catch him firmly by the collar. Lift him off the ground and shake him hard four times, saying "Whoa" harshly as you set him down. If the dog continues to jump in after several occasions for this discipline, the next time you catch him and lift him off the ground, give him a stinging lash on the belly.

Do not try to correct this fault with an electronic trainer used in the normal manner; the risk of making a blinker is too great. However, when conventional methods of discipline fail, there is a way that the electronic trainer can be used effectively with little risk. Put the electronic collar around the dog's flank in the manner described previously in the instructions for correcting catwalking. The collar should be tight enough so that the contact studs touch the dog's belly, but not so tight that it will impede his running.

Now course the dog into game with the transmitter ready. When you walk in to flush, and the dog moves to beat you to it, command "Whoa" and shock him. The dog will jump sideward or backward, but he will not quit pointing. There is no danger of causing blinking if you say "Whoa" as you shock. The dog does not associate the unpleasant sensation with the bird, as he is liable to if shocked in the normal place, forward on his neck. He associates the shock on his belly with something in the cover. He becomes reluctant to jump again for fear of being struck again. Two or three such experiences will make most dogs reliable on game.

There is yet another way of attacking this problem, but I recommend it only when other means fail. I do not recommend it at all for a field trial dog unless the handler is one who can accurately appraise his dog, and knows that the dog is hard-headed enough, and a strong enough pointer, that it will not mar his style on point.

The hunter willing to take the risk to keep his dog from spoiling shots may want to consider this method. Get a coil from a Model T and rig it to a switch and a 6-volt battery. Ground the coil and run a wire out thirty or forty feet to a likely spot of cover. Attach the wire to a small wire cage with a flip lid and a wooden bottom. Put a quail in the cage and work the dog upwind to the bird. Have a helper ready to operate the switch so that, when the dog points, you can walk in as you would to flush. When the dog jumps in, have the helper throw the switch, and the dog will get a shock on the nose as he tries to grab the bird. He will let out a yelp and back off, standing sheepishly or refusing to point. Don't try to make him point. Pet the dog; then lead or carry him off, and work your way back to the car. Put the dog away for the day and let him sleep on it.

It is a rare dog that will ever jump in to that cage again. Most dogs that have put a nose to it once will point wild birds without jumping in. They remember the lesson.

On the next few finds, avoid commanding "Whoa". The lesson has put the dog on the verge of blinking. Don't push him over the edge with voice commands. Let the dog stand for fear of jumping in, rather than from fear of you.

If you use this method, it is important that you put the dog away for the day after his experience with the cage. He's like a rider unnerved by a bad fall from a horse. If the rider climbs right back on he overcomes his fear; if he waits until another day, the fear of riding is hard for him to overcome.

For the strong pointing dog whose character has been properly judged, this method is sensational. On others it may leave its mark. Older dogs will take it better than younger ones, especially derbies. It is, in short, a method that should not be employed until you reach the point where you feel that you have little to lose if the fault cannot be corrected.

Seeing Birds on the Ground

This, like gunshyness, is a major fault created by owners, and like gunshyness, it is far easier to avoid than correct.

The villain in this case is the owner who is over-eager to see his puppy point a bird. A game bird or a pigeon, perhaps hobbled or crippled, is put out. The owner leads the dog to where the scent is obvious, and is greatly pleased when the dog points. He holds the dog on leash while he flushes the bird. It flies short, and he just has to see the puppy point again. The dog is now highly excited and jerking on his restraint. The owner, pulled by the lunging dog, follows the bird. The dog is no longer using his nose; he wants to catch that bird. Pointing has taken a back seat. If the puppy points at all this time, it is not until he can see the bird, and then only from instinct.

Not satisfied, the owner has to try it again another day, and it takes very few such expeditions to build into the puppy one of the worst faults a pointing dog can acquire. The dog will not point until he can see the game. Later, on wild birds, he will invariably approach so close that he will flush them. If the owner loses his temper at the dog's continual flushing and whips him, the probability is that the dog will become birdshy, or, at best, point with no more character than a sway-backed mule. This is a high price to pay for seeing a puppy point.

Once a puppy has learned to use his nose, avoid at all costs letting him see the bird on the ground.

If the trait has already been acquired by your dog, the best course of action is thorough and, if necessary, drastic retraining on "Whoa" so that you can stop him the moment he begins to make game. If you find that you can not accomplish this by conventional forms of discipline—lifting the dog off the ground by his collar and shaking him, or if necessary lifting him and applying *one* lash that really stings his belly—your best recourse is to use the electronic collar on his belly in the manner described under "Catwalking" and "Jumping In".

Wanting to see the bird is, of course, not the only reason that dogs flush birds. A good staunch dog can be fooled by wind currents, a fast dog can over-run his nose, and a young dog can slip back in training because of misadventures. On a covey rise there may be one quail wing-tipped from a previous hunt that flops back to earth. Or the dog is being trained without a check-cord and a bird flies short. The dog sees the bird rise and fall, breaks point and catches it. The next time he is on a bird he anticipates the same happening and rushes in.

Teach the fast dog the "Slow" command (see "Wildness after Frequent Finds"). The cure for the dog led astray by mishaps is to go back and retrain on staunchness (see Chapter 4).

Sulking after Correction

Like people who sulk, dogs that sulk and refuse to hunt after correction are a pain. Your first impulse is to stomp 'em good, but let your better sense take over. Patience is a necessity.

Think back about what you have done that could have caused the problem. Was your discipline overly severe? Did you jerk that training cord too hard for this dog? Did you whip the dog when a good shaking would have served the purpose? If you had to apply the lash, did you in anger strike him repeatedly, when one or two lashes that really sting applied with no display of temper would have served you better? If you did lose your temper, your angry voice may have compounded your felony; dogs are very perceptive of real anger and are cowed by it. Did you overdo the electronic trainer? Electronic discipline improperly used is a villain for this. Did you shock the dog too hard, too frequently, or too often in the same limited training area? Did you shock the dog as soon as you turned him loose in the field, without giving him a chance to work off steam? If your dog is not the kind that runs off, you have much to gain and nothing to lose in giving the dog a chance to settle down before you begin giving commands and applying discipline. If he is the kind that runs away on you, take him to an area where you won't have to worry about highways and other hazards in his absence, and wait for him to reappear before you put the pressure on.

But the damage has been done, now what? Working the sulky dog with a good biddable dog will help. Watching the other dog hunt may revive the sulker's interest. Get the dog involved with birds as quickly as possible to fire him up. Shut your eyes to mistakes he makes until his good nature returns. Then clamp down on discipline gradually.

If you can honestly say that you did nothing that would make the average dog sulk, you will probably have to treat the dog with kid gloves as long as you own him.

Slipping the Collar when Chained

Some dogs are very clever at this trick, but they can easily be foiled. Put two collars of equal size on the dog, and attach the chain to the inner collar. The outer collar keeps the inner collar from slipping over the head. Check the inner collar for excessive stretch every ten days for a month. Collars stretch considerably.

Don't use chain slip collars. They are dangerous to dog and man. The dog can choke himself, and a man can break his fingers when a rambunctious dog he is holding by the collar twists the chain.

Safety in an Open Truck

Some hunters without dog crates like their dogs to ride in the bed of their pick-up trucks. This of course is hazardous unless the

The "double collar" technique will cure a dog that slips its collar.

dog has been trained not to jump out until commanded to do so. Such training is not difficult.

Attach an eye-bolt or eye-screw in the truckbed 18 inches behind the cab and equidistant from each side of the truck. In some trucks this can be done by attaching a long two-by-three to existing body holes and inserting an eye screw in that. In others it may be necessary to drill the truck floor for an eye-bolt and plug the hole when no longer needed with a round-headed machine bolt.

Attach to the eye-bolt a cord with a snap. The cord should be just long enough to reach 20 inches above the ground directly opposite the eye on either side of the truck.

Lower the tail gate, put the dog in the truck, snap the cord to his collar, and close the tail gate. Walk off to the side forty feet and watch, without saying anything. The dog will soon get enough courage to jump over the side. Let him. Only his hind feet will touch the ground. He will be frightened, but he won't be hurt. There is no danger of injuring his neck, which is the toughest part of a dog's body.

When the dog is in this position, go to him, pick him up bodily and put him back in the truck, over the side without removing the cord.

Then stand back and again wait without saying anything. It is probable that the dog will not jump the second time, but if he does let him wait a little longer before you rescue him. Put him back over the side as before, and give him another chance to jump. If he does not, lower the tail gate, take the dog out, and put him in the kennel for the day.

The next day, repeat the procedure, giving the dog another chance to jump when fastened to the cord. When it appears that he has no intention to do so, unhook the cord and drive slowly down the road or around the block as a test of the training.

It is fright and the dog's instinct for self preservation that make the training effective, not the mild discomfort of the jerk from the rope.

It goes without saying that once the dog is trained, you must never put the dog in the truck or take him out without lowering the tail gate. If you invite him to jump out without lowering the gate he will be reluctant to come, and if you insist on his coming you will undo your training.

Night Barking Without Cause

A new dog in your kennel, especially a young dog, will bark because he is upset and wants attention. A dog allowed in the house during the day and kenneled at night may bark for much the same reason. Don't try to silence them by talking to them. That rewards their desire for attention, and will only lead to more barking.

With a new young dog, you should have patience within reason. He is like a youngster scared or uneasy in strange surroundings. If you have a dog box for your truck or station wagon or a shipping crate, put the dog in that. He is likely to quiet down. If it fails, and you can, put another dog in with him. If the box or crate is in your vehicle, take the dog for a ride for a mile or so and afterward let him sleep in the box.

The older dog that barks when put out at night can also often be silenced by shutting him in his kennel box.

But the dog persists in barking, and you have had enough. Get a glass of water and sneak up on him. When he opens his mouth to bark, let go with the water, and repeat as necessary. You may find that the sneaking up is the difficult part. Some dogs will sense your approach, even though you think you are quiet as a mouse. They will stop barking before you reach them, only to begin again as soon as you leave. If the dog barks enough to bring you out, apply the treatment anyway. Go to him in the dark, or with only a small flashlight so that you can see your way, say nothing and apply the water even though the dog is now silent. A few repetitions will establish the connection with his barking.

A variation of this treatment is to take along a dazzling 6-volt light. Leave it off until you get to the dog. Then shine it directly in his face, say "Quiet", and throw the water. The blinding light has a telling effect. Later, when he barks unnecessarily, shining the light toward him will generally bring silence.

Anti-bark collars are effective, but if you use one make sure it is not too tight. If too tight, the dog will get a heavy shock. The dog may panic and yelp loudly, bringing a second heavy shock right on top of the first. The collar should be loose enough so that the dog gets only a light shock.

A low-wattage light over the kennel area is effective in keeping dogs quiet at night, and has the added advantage of keeping vermin or stray animals away. A radio playing softly all night also has a generally soothing effect, but doesn't seem to do much for a newly acquired dog.

Parasites and Ailments

In handling dogs for many years, one learns the symptoms and treatment of common ailments. This does not entitle me to diagnose and prescribe for others, but some good general advice is in order.

Watch your dog for tell-tale symptoms of parasites or illness—loss of stamina, loss of appetite, runny nose, poor coat, poor or bloody stools, dragging his hindquarters ("sleigh-riding"), coughing, white segments in stools, abnormal thirst, abnormal change in tail carriage, etc. If any of these appear, get your dog to a qualified veterinarian for examination.

Have your dog blood-tested periodically for heartworm—at least once a year in cool climates, twice a year where mosquitoes are active much of the year. You may feel that you are in a heartworm-free area, but don't count on it. It used to be that heartworm was a problem only in the South. But present-day mobility of man and beast has spread the parasite far and wide. Today there can be a developing heart-worm problem anywhere there are mosquitoes and one infected dog. It is also a good idea from time to time to have the dog's stool examined for other internal parasites, and to keep your dog free of the external parasites that help to spread them.

Be sure to have your dog inoculated for distemper, hepatitis, leptospirosis and parvovilus, and keep up the booster shots. Have him vaccinated for rabies also.

These things will cost a few dollars, but it is a small price to pay for the privilege of having a fine bird dog.

6

More Things to Ponder

What Makes a Good Grouse Dog?

It takes three things to make a good grouse dog, one whose points you can shoot birds over:

1. The dog must lean on you for direction and companionship. This does not mean a dog that must be constantly handled. It means one that wants to know where you are at all times, and reports frequently to check your whereabouts.
2. He must work with a high head, picking up scent through the air at a goodly distance.
3. He must point far enough back so that he does not flush the nervous grouse. Once pointing, he must remain staunch, not taking that extra step that flushes the bird. If the bird runs and it is necessary to send the dog on, he should move at a speed logical to the cover.

The third requisite depends a good deal on the second. A low-headed foot trailer invariably waltzes into the grouse before he realizes it. Only rarely will a grouse hold for a dog that comes close.

The high headed dog with a good nose and the desire to work

for his handler has the makings of a great grouse dog. The rest depends on training and experience. If at all possible, train your dog on grouse. On liberated birds, all dogs have a tendency to point too close. Working on grouse will teach him to judge distance. If necessary to train on liberated birds, try to use birds that flush at the slightest provocation, and take your dog into good grouse cover whenever you can to broaden his experience.

I hear someone saying "I saw Grouse Champion Soandso run, and he came a long way from meeting your first requirement". Also you probably heard a lot of noisy voice-handling that you would not want to hear if you were out in the grouse woods with a gun. It is a strange thing that a grouse that will sit tight for a whistle or a dog bell will flush at the sound of the human voice.

Bear in mind that a grouse trial is mainly a field trial run in the woods. The winning dog is undoubtedly high in the second and third requirements if he finds and handles a grouse. Perhaps he also would have been high in the first requirement if he had been brought up to handle for a foot hunter out to shoot birds.

Should I Work My Dog in the Off Season?

For a fully trained dog, I don't recommend it until two or three weeks before the opening of the season, when you will want to begin hardening him for the work ahead. If you just can't resist the pleasure of working your dog in the field until then, at least be aware of its perils.

You won't have your shotgun to bring the act to a climax when your dog points. With no pellets whistling through the air, the birds probably won't fly as far and may land in a thicket. Being human, you will decide to work them again. Your dog will go into the heavy cover, and perhaps have a good point. You won't be able to see him, and in your light summer clothing will be reluctant to fight your way into the briars and tangle. You'll stand on the outside, hoping the dog will reappear, but he doesn't. If he's on point, sooner or later the bird or the dog will give. Usually it's the dog, and he moves. The bird flushes and the dog follows. It takes few such episodes for the dog to begin flushing deliberately when he scents game.

Further, it encourages your dog to seek heavy cover, from

which it will be difficult to call him when you want him to come. There is too much there to distract him.

If you were actually hunting, you would fight your way into the cover, no matter how tangled, shoot the bird when you found your dog on point, and then move on to a different locale.

Many a good pointing dog has been unhinged by too much off-season practicing.

When Should I Breed a Male Dog?

Preferably by the time he is two or at most not much over two-and-a-half. If a dog is not bred at least once while young, it frequently happens that when his stud service is wanted he lacks the desire and know-how. Stimulants to the sex glands are not always satisfactory.

Breeding a male too often has undesirable aspects, particularly if he is a house dog. He may get to think that sex is the most important thing in life and act accordingly.

Is Penning or Chaining Better?

My experience has been that the chained-out dog with his individual house is a more apt pupil in serious training than the dog that shares a kennel and pen with other dogs. The chained-out dog takes to discipline better. If he is timid, it makes him bold. Seldom does it fail to make a timid dog bouncy, and this is true of all breeds. The chain keeps the dog in better physical condition; when he lunges against it all his muscles are being employed. The chained dog is easier to leash to take to the field. If he runs around or shies away, you need only to step on the chain and walk on it until you reach and collar the dog.

The shortcomings of chaining out are that it requires more land area per dog and more work to keep the area neat and clean. A continuing watch must be kept on collars, which wear and stretch, and stakes occasionally pull out.

A good stake is a 22-inch bolt with a 2-inch solid washer at the top to enlarge the head. Slide a 1½-inch ring on the bolt and drive the bolt into the ground. Attach a 6-foot chain to the ring with a chain-repair link, and use another chain-repair link to attach

Recommended fittings for a stake-out chain. Left: security swivel snap. Center: Chain-repair link used to attach chain to snap and to stake ring. Right: "O" ring for dog's collar, a must if ordinary spring snaps are used.

a swivel snap to the dog's end of the chain. Use a snap of the type illustrated, sometimes called a "security" snap, in preference to a conventional spring snap or a bolt or slip snap. A spring snap will twist open, especially if hooked to the D-ring in the dog's collar. Anchored to the dog's collar, the D-ring cannot twist and turn with the snap. Instead of using the D-ring, slip an O-ring on the dog's collar and hook the snap to that. This is a must when a spring snap is used and a good idea with any type of snap. A bolt or slip snap is also to be avoided because it can catch dirt and slide open, particularly at night when the dog curls up.

The advantages of a kennel with a fenced-in run are that it is easier to maintain in appearance and cleanliness, and it requires less land area when several dogs are kept. It is practical for dry feeding, and provides more protection against theft. It is excellent for a dog that has completed training or before training begins.

Between chaining and penning, there is no noticeable difference in the contentment of the dog. Contentment for the dog lies in your attitude, not in his quarters.

How Did Bird Dog Training Become a Profession?

Once upon a time there was an affluent city man who loved hunting and heard tales about an area where the cover was great and the birds plentiful. It could have been in upper New England, or maybe in Georgia. Anyway, he decided to take his gun and his two dogs and find out for himself.

On arrival, he inquired at the village post office where he could find somebody to take him hunting. "Don't rightly know," the postmaster said, "Most folks here are too busy farming to hunt. You might try at Jeb Jones's store down at the forks and see if Abe Tracy's there. Abe never works, just fishes, traps, and hunts. Mebbe he'll take you."

At Jeb's store, the city man found Abe sitting by the potbelly stove. After introductions, Abe agreed to take him hunting the rest of the week. Abe had a couple of good bird dogs he had trained, and under Abe's tutelage the young dogs of the city man, let's call him Mr. Smith, developed rapidly. When the time came to go home, it occurred to Mr. Smith that it would be a good idea to leave his dogs with Abe for further experience. Abe said, "Sure", and chained the dogs out back.

Mr. Smith was not the only city hunter to come by that Fall. A few days later Mr. Cannon showed up, and before the season ended, several others followed under similar circumstances. By one means or another, all found their way to Abe, and enjoyed good hunting and watching their dogs develop. Soon Abe had a dozen extra dogs chained up around his place. Thanks to payments for training, Abe had more money in his pocket than ever before, but otherwise he hadn't changed a bit. He could be more often found regaling cronies with his tales in front of Jeb Jones's potbelly stove than out working his new charges.

This wouldn't have surprised their well-to-do owners very much. They never expected Abe to overwork himself. Old-timers reading this will laugh and say, "It was just like that, but I didn't mind. I had a good time and the best hunting ever."

Times have changed. The companionship of city men and the likes of Abe Tracy has mostly disappeared. Changes in agricultural methods, shrinkage of hunting cover and the supply of wild birds, the introduction of liberated birds and changes in training techniques, all add up to the sorrow of the old-fashioned natural bird dog and the laissez-faire attitude that went with the era. Today's professional trainer is a far cry from Abe Tracy.

Some of today's successful professionals began as successful amateurs. They enjoyed success with their own dogs and went on to train for others, learning from mistakes and growing and improving with experience. But there are pitfalls in this road. Dogs vary greatly in ability and temperament. The budding professional may learn to his sorrow and that of others that the approach that worked well with his dogs does harm rather than good to some of the dogs brought to him.

It would be well for the aspiring professional to serve an apprenticeship with a good veteran professional until he has broader knowledge of all of the multitude of problems he will encounter and of ways of handling those problems.

Does a Trainer Leave His Signature on a Dog?

If you study a score or more of the dogs trained by a first-class professional trainer, you will consistently see dogs with beautifully polished manners and absolutely no loss of style or character. On the other hand, you may study an equal number of dogs developed by another trainer with equally long experience and frequently see dogs that flag, drop on point, or lose character as the handler approaches. The trainer himself may be aware of this but unable to analyze his weaknesses.

Some trainers excel on certain phases of a dog's development, but fail on other phases. Some trainers have great success with extroverted dogs but not with introverts; with other trainers, the picture is reversed. Whether you live North, South, East or West, if you will study the prominent trainers in your area you will reach your own conclusions on the character of the dogs with which they are most successful.

Many leading field-trial trainers lean toward strains of dogs that fit their individualities and methods. They have learned to recognize the traits that characterize dogs they will do well with, and stay on this course. If trainers fail to do this, or fail to analyze themselves and their methods, they never reach full potential.

Do You Recommend Dog Training as a Career?

The professional dog trainer has rewards that can't be deposited at the bank. Seeing his dogs perform well brings a thrill and inner satisfaction. He meets and makes friends with people in all walks and stations of life. He has plenty of hard work to develop him physically, and derives health and happiness from an outdoor occupation.

On the other hand, he is on 24-hour call, seven days a week.

There is constant concern about the welfare of his dogs and the satisfaction of his clients. His income tends to be seasonal, but his overhead is year around and disproportionately heavy.

If—like the man who loves horses so much that the aroma of the stable is an exciting perfume—you love bird dogs so much that you never want to be far from a dog on point, you might consider dog training as a career. But if you have a big family to support, are practical or mercenary, you had better seek a more lucrative vocation.